MACARON MAGIC 2

Individual Desserts and Showpieces

MACARON MAGIC 2

Individual Desserts and Showpieces

Jialin Tian, Ph.D.

Photographs and Design by Jialin Tian
Step-by-Step Photographs by Yabin Yu

Macaron Magic 2: Individual Desserts and Showpieces

Jialin Tian, Ph.D.

Published in the United States by
Jayca Inc.
P. O. Box 2451
Poquoson, VA 23662
USA

Photographs and styling: Jialin Tian
Step-by-step photographs and author's photographs: Yabin Yu
Book design, layout, and illustrations: Jialin Tian
Production manager: Yabin Yu

www.macaronmagic.com

ISBN 978-0-9837764-2-0

First Edition

To my mother, Yabin

CONTENTS

INTRODUCTION

Almonds, sugar, egg whites, and magic! Encore! In this second installment of *Macaron Magic*, we explore the tantalizing world of individual desserts and showpieces for macarons. Individual desserts, or petits gâteaux, are small individual-portion-size cakes with multiple components, such as layers of biscuits, sponge cakes, or macaron shells, cream, mousse, or fruit fillings, and something crunchy to enhance the texture. Adorned with intricately designed decorations, these jewel-box-like edible works of art are absolute delights! In this book, we focus on the techniques of using the macaron as one component of individual desserts. Macaron towers are dazzling showpieces composed of colorful macaron arrangements, usually in pyramid shapes. In the first volume of *Macaron Magic*, we discussed the techniques to construct a macaron tower. In this book, we venture away from the traditional tower shape and present macaron showpieces in the tier forms often seen in cakes. In addition to its uniqueness, one advantage of building a macaron showpiece in tiers is that you can easily attach decorations to it.

This book is divided into six chapters. The first four chapters are inspired by seasonal color palettes and ingredients. We present twelve innovative creations of macaron desserts, including pineapple and ibérico ham, Meyer lemon and hazelnut, white peach and white chocolate, walnut, fig, and chocolate, and more. Each of these four chapters also includes step-by-step photography-guided instructions on how to build a spectacular showpiece using the seasonal color palette. Chapter Five contains the basic recipes that are used throughout the book. In the bonus chapter, we present advanced techniques for creating stunning chocolate and pulled sugar decorations. Although these decorations are optional for macaron desserts and showpieces, mastering the skills needed to create them can help you enhance the visual impact of these edible works of art.

Macaron Magic 2 introduces techniques for creating professional-quality macaron desserts and showpieces as well as advanced decorating methods. Recipes are accompanied by step-by-step photographs to demonstrate procedures, construction diagrams to offer quick assembly references, and photographs of finished desserts to provide inspiration.

It was an absolute joy to create the second volume of *Macaron Magic*. My deepest appreciation goes to my mother Yabin. She is responsible for taking thousands of step-by-step photographs; her diligent work has brought the intricate procedures described in this book to life. Many thanks to my father Richard, for all of his help and sacrifices during the making of this book. I want to thank Chefs Jacquy Pfeiffer and Sébastien Canonne at the French Pastry School in Chicago for their support, encouragement, and recognition. Many thanks go to Chef Stéphane Glacier for his support. My appreciation to the chefs and instructors whom I met during my adventurous pastry-making years; I wish to thank them for their friendship and for sharing their knowledge and experience with me. Finally, my sincere gratitude to my readers! When I first started writing *Macaron Magic*, I never would have imagined the enthusiastic comments and feedback that I have received. Without the support of my readers, I would not have had the courage or motivation to start on this second book. I hope this book will bring you endless enjoyment!

SPRING

SPRING

LYCHEE AND RASPBERRY

Lychee fruit has been an exquisite Chinese delicacy for centuries. Once enjoyed only by the royalty of ancient China, lychee fruit has been mentioned in legends and poems, and depicted in artwork. When I was young, my grandmother taught me a poem by the famous poet Du Mu who lived during the late Tang Dynasty, around the 9th century. Yang Guifei was Emperor Xuanzong's beloved consort and one of the legendary beauties of ancient China. Guifei's love for lychees was well known. The poem portrayed the imperial messengers who were reserved for urgent military missions dashing through the gates of the capital city on speedy horses, but no one knew they were making an express delivery of fresh lychees that put a smile on Guifei's face. Of course, the poem has a sarcastic overtone. I was five when my grandmother read it to me; at the time, I was less concerned with the political implication of the poem and more concerned with having some juicy, fresh lychees after my study session.

Lychee has a reddish rind with a rough texture. On the inside, the white translucent flesh is sweet, juicy, and tender with an oval-shaped hard core in the center. The flavor is unique but not as pronounced as some other tropical fruits. Lychees can be found in most gourmet stores; most lychees sold in the United States are cultivated in California and Florida.

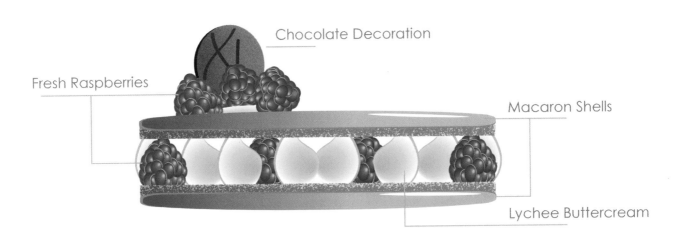

Chocolate Decoration

Fresh Raspberries

Macaron Shells

Lychee Buttercream

Yield: 6 to 8 4-in/10.2-cm diameter individual desserts

INGREDIENTS

Macaron Shells:

1 recipe Macaron Shells (page 82)

0.014 oz/0.4 g red powdered food coloring

Lychee Buttercream:

0.088 oz/2.5 g sheet gelatin (silver grade) or 0.074 oz/2.1 g powdered gelatin + 0.44 oz/12.6 g cold water

6.7 oz/190 g lychee puree

0.42 oz/12 g cornstarch

0.42 oz/12 g lychee liqueur (optional)

10.58 oz/300 g Swiss meringue buttercream (page 86)

Assembly and Decoration:

Fresh raspberries

Powdered sugar for dusting

Chocolate decorations (page 90)

Macaron Shells:

1. Follow the directions on page 82 to make the batter for macaron shells. Add powdered food coloring if desired.

2. To make the large macaron shell disks, fill a large pastry bag (18 in/45.7 cm) fitted with a 0.38-in/1-cm plain tip with the macaron batter, and pipe a 3.5-in/8.9-cm disk by making a spiral coil on the silicone baking mat (1). The batter will spread out to about 4 in/10.2 cm in diameter. Repeat to pipe more shells (2).

3. Gently tap the baking pan against a hard surface to reduce air bubbles in the batter. Use a toothpick to pop any remaining air bubbles. Bake the macaron shells at 320°F/160°C for about 16 to 18 minutes.

Lychee Buttercream:

1. In a medium-sized bowl, bloom the sheet gelatin in plenty of cold water. If powdered gelatin is used, sprinkle the powder over 0.44 oz/12.6 g cold water in the bowl. Let the gelatin bloom for at least 10 minutes before use.

2. Combine the lychee puree with cornstarch in a medium-sized stainless steel saucepan (3). Mix well with a balloon whisk. Bring the mixture to a boil over medium-high heat while whisking constantly (4). Remove from heat when the mixture thickens (5). Let cool slightly.

3. Meanwhile, squeeze excess water out of the bloomed sheet gelatin and add the gelatin to the lychee mixture (6). If powdered gelatin is used, add the entire content to the lychee mixture. Mix in the lychee liqueur if desired (7). Stir to combine. Let cool slightly. Cover the surface of the lychee mixture with plastic wrap.

4. When the mixture has cooled completely, combine it with Swiss meringue buttercream (page 86) in a mixer bowl. Beat with a stand mixer fitted with

a wire whisk attachment on high speed until the lychee buttercream is light, fluffy, and well combined (**8**).

Assembly and Decoration:

1. Fill a large piping bag (18 in/45.7 cm) fitted with a large plain tip (0.5 in/1.3 cm) with lychee buttercream.

2. Place a macaron disk on a clean surface with its smooth side down. Pipe dollops of cream along the outer edge of the macaron disk while leaving some space between neighboring dollops of cream (**9**). Pipe more cream in the center of the disk (**10**).

3. Place fresh raspberries along the edge between dollops of cream and in the center (**11, 12**). Pipe more cream on top of the raspberries (**13**). Cover the filling with another macaron disk with its smooth side up.

4. Pipe a dollop of cream on top of the pastry; arrange more raspberries around the cream (**14**). Dust the berries with powdered sugar (**15**). Finish decorating the dessert with a chocolate disk placed behind the berries (**16**).

PINEAPPLE AND IBÉRICO HAM

This dessert is inspired by the classic combination of pineapple and ham, but with a unique twist. One of my favorite dry-cured hams is the jamón ibérico de bellota of Spain. The ibérico ham is produced from free-roaming acorn-fed black Iberian pigs. The meat is sweet, nutty, slightly gamey, and highly addictive! Last winter I bought a whole ibérico ham for my mother as her Christmas present. We planned to savor the ham for several months, but there were only bits and pieces left after about a week's snacking. The crispy cracklings made from the fatty ham pieces were absolutely delicious, especially when sprinkled on top of the sweet, creamy pineapple filling. You can substitute the ibérico ham fat with fat from serrano or prosciutto ham, or even crispy bacon.

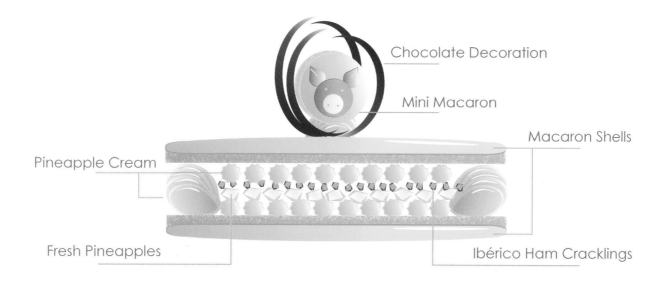

Chocolate Decoration

Mini Macaron

Macaron Shells

Pineapple Cream

Fresh Pineapples

Ibérico Ham Cracklings

Yield: 6 to 8 4-in/10.2-cm diameter individual desserts

Ingredients

Macaron Shells:

1 recipe Macaron Shells (page 82)

0.0035 oz/0.1 g white + 0.0035 oz/0.1 g yellow powdered food coloring

Pineapple Cream:

0.088 oz/2.5 g sheet gelatin (silver grade) or 0.074 oz/2.1 g powdered gelatin + 0.44 oz/12.6 g cold water

1.76 oz/50 g egg yolks

1.76 oz/50 g granulated sugar

1.06 oz/30 g cornstarch

8.82 oz/250 g pineapple puree

0.71 oz/20 g unsalted butter, at room temperature (A)

7.05 oz/200 g unsalted butter, at room temperature (B)

Ibérico Ham Cracklings:

7.05oz/200 g ibérico ham fat

Assembly and Decoration:

Fresh pineapple pieces, cut into 0.25-in/0.6-cm cubes

Mini macarons

Chocolate decorations (page 90)

Macaron Shells:

1. Follow the directions on page 82 to make the batter for macaron shells. Add powdered food coloring if desired.

2. To make the large macaron shell disks, fill a large pastry bag (18 in/45.7 cm) fitted with a 0.38-in/1-cm plain tip with the macaron batter, and pipe a 3.5-in/8.9-cm disk by making a spiral coil on the silicone baking mat (1). The batter will spread out to about 4 in/10.2 cm in diameter. Repeat to pipe more shells (2).

3. Gently tap the baking pan against a hard surface to reduce air bubbles in the batter. Use a toothpick to pop any remaining air bubbles. Bake the macaron shells at 320°F/160°C for about 16 to 18 minutes.

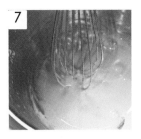

4. Reserve some batter to pipe a half-sheet pan of mini macaron shells 1.25 in/3.2 cm in diameter (3). If desired, make a pig design on top of each shell before baking. Fill a small pastry bag fitted with a small plain tip with pink-colored macaron batter. Pipe two small dots and one big dot on each macaron shell to represent the ears and face (4). Switch back to the original yellow-colored batter and pipe a dot in the middle of the big pink dot (face) to indicate the snout (5). Use a toothpick to make the eyes, ear tips, and nostrils (6). Bake the mini macaron shells at 325°F/163°C for about 11 minutes.

Pineapple Cream:

1. In a medium-sized bowl, bloom the sheet gelatin in plenty of cold water. If powdered gelatin is used, sprinkle the powder over 0.44 oz/12.6 g cold water in the bowl. Let the gelatin bloom for at least 10 minutes before use.

2. Combine egg yolks, granulated sugar, and cornstarch in a stainless steel mixing bowl. Mix well with a balloon whisk (7). Set aside.

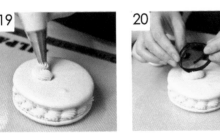

3. Heat the pineapple puree in a medium-sized stainless steel saucepan over medium-high heat **(8)**. Remove from heat when the puree comes to a boil. Pour about half of the puree into the reserved egg yolk mixture while whisking vigorously. Pour the entire mixture back into the pan. Cook the mixture over medium-low heat while whisking constantly for about one to two minutes until the mixture thickens **(9)**. Let cool slightly. Stir in the first portion of soft butter (A).

4. Meanwhile, squeeze excess water out of the bloomed sheet gelatin and add the gelatin to the pineapple mixture **(10)**. If powdered gelatin is used, add the entire content to the pineapple mixture. Stir to combine. Let cool slightly. Cover the surface of the pineapple mixture with plastic wrap.

5. Place the mixture in a mixer bowl when it has cooled completely. Attach the bowl to a stand mixer fitted with a wire whisk attachment. Whisk in the soft butter (B) in small increments at medium-low speed. Make sure each addition of butter is thoroughly incorporated before adding more butter. Scrape down the sides of the bowl with a spatula if necessary.

6. Once all of the butter is incorporated, adjust the mixer to medium-high speed. Continue to beat for a few more minutes until the pineapple cream is light and fluffy **(11)**.

Ibérico Ham Cracklings:

1. Cut the ham fat into small cubes and place them in a stainless steel saucepan **(12)**. Cook the cubes over medium-high heat. Stir occasionally. Render the fat until the cubes are golden and crispy **(13)**.

2. Drain excess fat using a strainer. The cracklings should weigh about ¼ of their original weight. Let cool completely.

Assembly and Decoration:

1. Fill a large piping bag (18 in/45.7 cm) fitted with a medium-sized star tip (0.31 in/0.8 cm) with pineapple cream.

2. Place a macaron disk on a clean surface with its smooth side down. Pipe dollops of cream along the outer edge of the macaron disk and in the center of the disk **(14, 15)**.

3. Place fresh pineapple cubes in the center **(16)**, followed by ham cracklings **(17)**, and top with more cream **(18)**. Cover the filling with another macaron disk with its smooth side up.

4. Pipe a dollop of cream on top of the pastry **(19)**. Decorate with a mini macaron and chocolate curls **(20)**.

COCONUT, BASIL, LIME, AND COCOA NIBS

Nothing can bring you out of the cold, dreary winter better than this light and refreshing tropical dessert. A hint of fresh basil introduces an interesting dimension to the sweet and citrusy combination of coconut and lime. The addition of rum-flavored cocoa nibs adds a crunchy texture to the dessert. Cocoa nibs are roasted and cracked cocoa beans with their husks removed. Cocoa nibs are the raw material for making chocolates. In their purest form, cocoa nibs are bitter, crunchy, and packed with the intense flavor of dark chocolate.

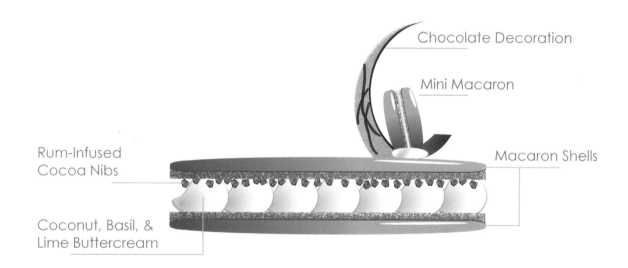

Chocolate Decoration

Mini Macaron

Rum-Infused
Cocoa Nibs

Macaron Shells

Coconut, Basil, &
Lime Buttercream

Yield: 12 5-in x 1.5-in/12.7-cm x 3.8-cm individual desserts

Macaron Shells:

1 recipe Macaron Shells (page 82)

0.007 oz/0.2 g yellow + 0.0018 oz/0.05 g green powdered food coloring

Coconut, Basil, and Lime Buttercream

0.088 oz/2.5 g sheet gelatin (silver grade) or 0.074 oz/2.1 g powdered gelatin + 0.44 oz/12.6 g cold water

7.76 oz/220 g coconut puree

0.42 oz/12 g lime juice

0.18 oz/5 g fresh lime zest from about 2 medium-sized limes

0.35 oz/10 g fresh basil leaves

0.42 oz/12 g cornstarch

10.58 oz/300 g Swiss meringue buttercream (page 86)

Rum-Infused Cocoa Nibs:

1.76 oz/50 g cocoa nibs

0.35 oz/10 g granulated sugar

0.35 oz/10 g dark rum

Assembly and Decoration:

Mini macarons

Chocolate decorations (page 90)

Macaron Shells:

1. Follow the directions on page 82 to make the batter for macaron shells. Add powdered food coloring if desired.

2. To make the long macaron shells, fill a large pastry bag (18 in/45.7 cm) fitted with a 0.38-in/1-cm plain tip with the macaron batter, and pipe a 4.5-in/11.4-cm long strip on the silicone baking mat; pipe another strip of batter directly on top of the first strip to double the volume. The batter will spread out to about 5 in/12.7 cm in length and 1.5 in/3.8 cm in width. Repeat to pipe more shells (**1, 2**).

3. Gently tap the baking pan against a hard surface to reduce air bubbles in the batter. Use a toothpick to pop any remaining air bubbles (**3**). Bake the macaron shells at 320°F/160°C for about 15 minutes (**4**).

4. Reserve some batter to pipe a half-sheet pan of mini macaron shells 1.25 in/3.2 cm in diameter (**5, 6**). Bake the mini macaron shells at 325°F/163°C for about 11 minutes.

Coconut, Basil, and Lime Buttercream:

1. In a medium-sized bowl, bloom the sheet gelatin in plenty of cold water. If powdered gelatin is used, sprinkle the powder over 0.44 oz/12.6 g cold water in the bowl. Let the gelatin bloom for at least 10 minutes before use.

2. Place the coconut puree, lime juice, lime zest, and basil leaves in a medium-sized stainless steel saucepan (**7**). Bring the mixture to a boil over medium-high heat (**8**). Remove from heat; cover the pan and allow the mixture to infuse for about 20 minutes.

3. Strain the mixture into a mixing bowl to remove the aromatics (**9**). Place the infused coconut puree back into the pan and stir in the cornstarch. Mix well with a balloon whisk. Bring the mixture to a

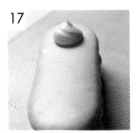

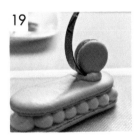

boil over medium-high heat while whisking constantly. Remove from heat when the mixture thickens (**10**). Let cool slightly.

4. Meanwhile, squeeze excess water out of the bloomed sheet gelatin and add the gelatin to the infused coconut mixture. If powdered gelatin is used, add the entire content to the infused coconut mixture. Stir to combine. Let cool slightly. Cover the surface of the mixture with plastic wrap.

5. When the mixture has cooled completely, combine it with Swiss meringue buttercream (page 86) in a mixer bowl. Beat with a stand mixer fitted with a wire whisk attachment on high speed until the coconut, basil, and lime buttercream is light, fluffy, and well combined (**11**).

Rum-Infused Cocoa Nibs:

1. Line a baking pan with parchment paper or silicone baking mat. In a small bowl, combine cocoa nibs, sugar, and dark rum. Mix well. Spread the mixture on the baking pan using a spoon (**12**).

2. Bake the rum-sugar-infused cocoa nibs in a 250°F/121°C oven for about 20 minutes. Let cool and set aside.

Assembly and Decoration:

1. Fill a large piping bag (18 in/45.7 cm) fitted with a medium-sized plain tip (0.38-in/1-cm) with coconut, basil, and lime buttercream.

2. Place a macaron strip on a clean surface with its smooth side down. Pipe dollops of cream in two parallel rows on the macaron strip (**13, 14**). Sprinkle rum-sugar-infused cocoa nibs on top of the cream (**15**). Cover the filling with another macaron strip with its smooth side up (**16**).

3. Pipe a dollop of cream on top of the pastry (**17**) and decorate with a mini macaron (**18**). Finish decorating the dessert with a chocolate leaf placed around the mini macaron (**19**).

SPRING SHOWPIECE

When I think of spring, I think of pink, pale yellow, green, and lavender. This macaron showpiece embraces the pastel palette of spring. The chocolate decorations enhance the showpiece with lively and youthful accents.

Macarons:

4 recipes Macaron Shells (page 82)

0.0035 oz/0.1 g yellow powdered food coloring

0.0035 oz/0.1 g red powdered food coloring

0.0035 oz/0.1 g green powdered food coloring

0.0035 oz/0.1 g blue + 0.0018 oz/0.05 g red powdered food coloring

Fillings for 4 recipes of macaron shells

Showpiece Structure:

1 14-in x 4-in/35.6-cm x 10.2-cm round Styrofoam disk (bottom tier)

1 10-in x 4-in/25.4-cm x 10.2-cm round Styrofoam disk (middle tier)

1 5-in/12.7-cm Styrofoam cube (top tier)

White drawing paper

Double-sided tape

Wooden toothpicks with two sharp ends

Nontoxic glue for arts and crafts

1 12-in x 9-in x 0.5-in/30.5-cm x 22.9-cm x 1.3-cm rectangular wooden board

Macarons:

1. Follow the directions on page 82 to make four recipes of 1.5-in/3.8-cm macaron shells. Use yellow, red, green, and purple (blue + red) powdered food coloring in the batter to make four different colored macaron shells (**1–4**).

2. Fill the macaron shells with the fillings of your choice (**5**). The fillings should have a consistency that is neither too soft nor too hard. If the filling is too soft, the macarons will become soggy and fall off the showpiece structure; on the other hand, if the filling is too hard, it will be difficult to attach the macarons to the toothpicks.

Showpiece Structure:

1. Cover the Styrofoam pieces with drawing paper using double-sided tape (**6**).

2. Insert toothpicks on one side of the middle tier Styrofoam disk (**7**). Apply a small amount of glue in the center of the bottom tier disk (**8**). Place the middle tier, with the toothpicks pointing downward, on top of the bottom tier and press down to stack the two layers. Repeat to stack the top tier (**9**).

3. For easy transport and enhanced stability, glue the supporting wooden board to the bottom of the lowest tier disk (**10**).

Assembly and Decoration:

1. Use a sharp needle to pierce a small hole in the bottom tier (**11**). Insert a toothpick at the marked

Assembly and Decoration:

Sharp needle

Wooden toothpicks with two sharp ends

Chocolate decorations (page 90)

Tempered dark chocolate (page 90)

Parchment paper cornet

Cooling spray for sugar and chocolate

location at an 80° to 90° angle with respect to the surface of interest (12), leaving about 0.25-in/0.6-cm to 0.5-in/1.3-cm of the toothpick outside. If the toothpick is too long, cut it in half and insert the cut side into the Styrofoam. Attach a macaron to the toothpick (13).

2. Repeat the process to attach more macarons to the supporting structure (14). Each tier consists of three rows of macarons. If necessary, use a ruler as a guide to align the macarons. Arrange the macarons in alternating colors (15).

3. To decorate the showpiece with chocolate spheres and leaves (page 90), put tempered chocolate into a parchment paper cornet, apply a small amount of chocolate on the back of a leaf (16), and attach it to the showpiece. If desired, spray the attaching joint with cooling liquid to solidify the chocolate instantly (17). Repeat to add more chocolate decorations.

5
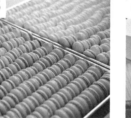

6

7
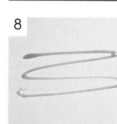

8
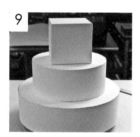

9
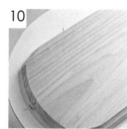

10

11
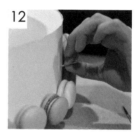

12

13

14

15

16

17
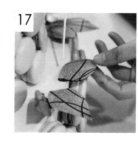

SUMMER

SUMMER

PASSION FRUIT AND MANGO

I love the bright, pungent flavor of passion fruit, but the fruit is too acidic to be enjoyed by itself. The addition of mango puree brings a sweet and fruity note to this intoxicating tropical blend.

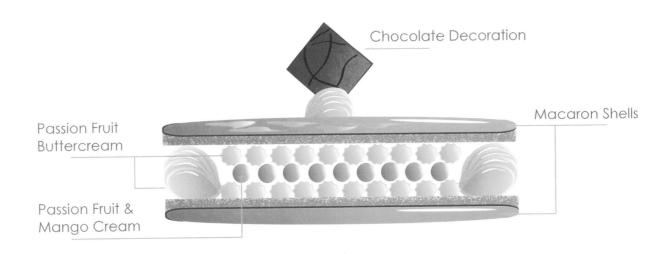

Chocolate Decoration

Macaron Shells

Passion Fruit Buttercream

Passion Fruit & Mango Cream

Yield: 6 to 8 4-in/10.2-cm diameter individual desserts

INGREDIENTS

Macaron Shells:

1 recipe Macaron Shells (page 82)

0.021 oz/0.6 g yellow + 0.0018 oz/0.05 g red powdered food coloring

Passion Fruit Buttercream:

0.13 oz/3.8 g sheet gelatin (silver grade) or 0.11 oz/3.2 g powdered gelatin + 0.67 oz/19.2 g cold water

3.53 oz/100 g whole eggs

2.29 oz/65 g granulated sugar

2.82 oz/80 g passion fruit puree

1.41 oz/40 g unsalted butter, at room temperature

10.58 oz/300 g Swiss meringue buttercream (page 86)

Passion Fruit and Mango Cream:

0.13 oz/3.8 g sheet gelatin (silver grade) or 0.11 oz/3.2 g powdered gelatin + 0.67 oz/19.2 g cold water

3.53 oz/100 g passion fruit puree

7.05 oz/200 g mango puree

1.76 oz/50 g granulated sugar

0.63 oz/18 g cornstarch

Assembly and Decoration:

Chocolate decorations (page 90)

Macaron Shells:

1. Follow the directions on page 82 to make the batter for macaron shells. Add powdered food coloring if desired.

2. To make the large macaron shell disks, fill a large pastry bag (18 in/45.7 cm) fitted with a 0.38-in/1-cm plain tip with the macaron batter, and pipe a 3.5-in/8.9-cm disk by making a spiral coil on the silicone baking mat (1). The batter will spread out to about 4 in/10.2 cm in diameter. Repeat to pipe more shells (2).

3. To make the heart designs, before baking the macaron shells, fill a small pastry bag fitted with a small plain tip with red-colored macaron batter. Pipe a few small dots along a curve on each macaron shell (3). Use a toothpick to make the hearts (4, 5).

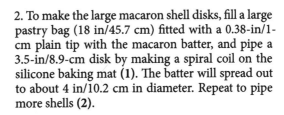

4. Gently tap the baking pan against a hard surface to reduce air bubbles in the batter. Use a toothpick to pop any remaining air bubbles. Bake the macaron shells at 320°F/160°C for about 16 to 18 minutes (6).

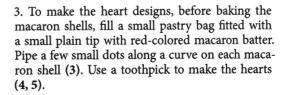

Passion Fruit Buttercream:

1. In a medium-sized bowl, bloom the sheet gelatin in plenty of cold water. If powdered gelatin is used, sprinkle the powder over 0.67 oz/19.2 g cold water in the bowl. Let the gelatin bloom for at least 10 minutes before use.

2. Combine eggs and granulated sugar in a stainless steel mixing bowl. Mix well with a balloon whisk. Set aside.

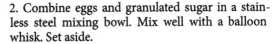

3. Heat the passion fruit puree in a medium-sized stainless steel saucepan over medium-high heat (7). Remove from heat when the puree comes to a boil. Pour about half of the puree into the reserved egg mixture while whisking vigorously (8). Pour the entire mixture back into the pan. Cook the mixture over medium-low heat while whisking constantly

for about one to two minutes until the mixture thickens (9). Let cool slightly. Stir in the butter and mix well (10).

4. Meanwhile, squeeze excess water out of the bloomed sheet gelatin and add the gelatin to the passion fruit mixture (11). If powdered gelatin is used, add the entire content to the passion fruit mixture. Stir to combine. Let cool slightly. Cover the surface of the passion fruit mixture with plastic wrap.

5. When the mixture has cooled completely, combine it with Swiss meringue buttercream (page 86) in a mixer bowl. Beat with a stand mixer fitted with a wire whisk attachment on high speed until the passion fruit buttercream is light, fluffy, and well combined (12).

Passion Fruit and Mango Cream:

1. In a medium-sized bowl, bloom the sheet gelatin in plenty of cold water. If powdered gelatin is used, sprinkle the powder over 0.67 oz/19.2 g cold water in the bowl. Let the gelatin bloom for at least 10 minutes before use.

2. Combine the passion fruit puree, mango puree, granulated sugar, and cornstarch in a medium-sized stainless steel saucepan. Mix well with a balloon whisk. Bring the mixture to a boil over medium-high heat while whisking constantly (13). Remove from heat when the mixture thickens (14). Let cool slightly.

3. Meanwhile, squeeze excess water out of the bloomed sheet gelatin and add the gelatin to the passion fruit-mango mixture (15). If powdered gelatin is used, add the entire content to the passion fruit-mango mixture. Stir to combine (16). Let cool slightly. Cover the surface of the passion fruit-mango cream with plastic wrap. Let cool completely.

Assembly and Decoration:

1. Fill a large piping bag (18 in/45.7 cm) fitted with a medium-sized star tip (0.31 in/0.8 cm) with passion fruit buttercream. Place a macaron disk on a clean surface with its smooth side down. Pipe dollops of buttercream along the outer edge of the macaron disk and in the center of the disk (17–19).

2. Fill a medium-sized piping bag (12 in/30.5 cm) fitted with a medium-sized plain tip (0.31 in/0.8 cm) with passion fruit-mango cream; pipe some cream in the center (20).

3. Switch back to the large pastry bag filled with passion fruit buttercream and pipe another layer of buttercream in the center (21). Cover the filling with another macaron disk with its smooth side up (22). Pipe a dollop of cream on top of the pastry (23). Finish decorating the dessert with a chocolate square (24).

WHITE PEACH AND WHITE CHOCOLATE

White peach is one of my favorite fruits. Sweet, juicy, and tender white peaches combined with white chocolate cream make an elegant summer dessert. A glass of refreshing Bellini made from white peach puree and Prosecco is the perfect complement to this delightful pastry.

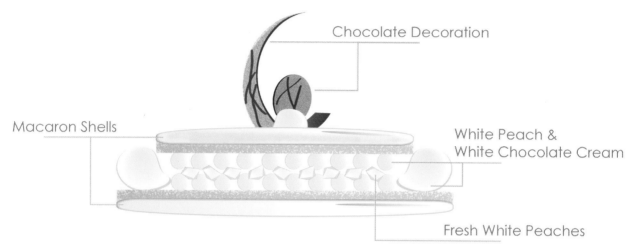

Chocolate Decoration

Macaron Shells

White Peach & White Chocolate Cream

Fresh White Peaches

Yield: 6 to 8 4-in/10.2-cm diameter individual desserts

Macaron Shells:

1 recipe Macaron Shells (page 82)

0.007 oz/0.2 g white powdered food coloring

0.007 oz/0.2 g red luster dust food coloring

0.042 oz/1.2 g vodka

White Peach and White Chocolate Cream:

0.088 oz/2.5 g sheet gelatin (silver grade) or 0.074 oz/2.1 g powdered gelatin + 0.44 oz/12.6 g cold water

8.11 oz/230 g white peach puree

0.42 oz/12 g cornstarch

4.23 oz/120 g white chocolate couverture, finely chopped

3.52 oz/100 g unsalted butter, at room temperature

Assembly and Decoration:

Fresh white peaches, finely diced

Chocolate decorations (page 90)

Macaron Shells:

1. Follow the directions on page 82 to make the batter for macaron shells. Add white powdered food coloring if desired.

2. To make the bottom (larger) macaron shell disks, fill a large pastry bag (18 in/45.7 cm) fitted with a 0.38-in/1-cm plain tip with the macaron batter, and pipe a 3.5-in/8.9-cm disk by making a spiral coil on the silicone baking mat (1). The batter will spread out to about 4 in/10.2 cm in diameter. Repeat to pipe more shells (2, 3).

3. Gently tap the baking pan against a hard surface to reduce air bubbles in the batter. Use a toothpick to pop any remaining air bubbles. Bake the bottom macaron shells at 320°F/160°C for about 16 to 18 minutes.

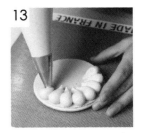

4. To make the top macaron shell disks with a smaller diameter, pipe a 2.75-in/7-cm disk by making a spiral coil on the silicone baking mat (4). The batter will spread out to about 3 in/7.6 cm in diameter. Repeat to pipe more shells (5). Bake the top macaron shells at 320°F/160°C for about 16 minutes (6).

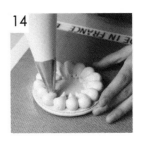

5. Allow the top macaron shells to cool completely. Mix the red luster dust with vodka. Lightly airbrush the top macaron shells (smaller disks) with the luster color mixture so that they resemble the appearance of a white peach (7).

Note: If an airbrush is not available, you can apply the luster dust mixture with a clean brush; reduce the amount of vodka if a paint brush is used.

White Peach and White Chocolate Cream:

1. In a medium-sized bowl, bloom the sheet gelatin in plenty of cold water. If powdered gelatin is used, sprinkle the powder over 0.44 oz/12.6 g cold water in the bowl. Let the gelatin bloom for at least 10 minutes before use.

2. Combine the white peach puree with cornstarch in a medium-sized stainless steel saucepan. Mix well with a balloon whisk. Bring the mixture to a boil over medium-high heat while whisking constantly **(8)**. Remove from heat when the mixture thickens. Add the white peach puree mixture to the white chocolate pieces and mix well **(9, 10)**.

3. Meanwhile, squeeze excess water out of the bloomed sheet gelatin and add the gelatin to the white peach-chocolate mixture **(11)**. If powdered gelatin is used, add the entire content to the white peach-chocolate mixture. Stir to combine. Let cool slightly. Cover the surface of the mixture with plastic wrap.

4. Place the white peach-chocolate mixture in a mixer bowl when it has cooled completely. Attach the bowl to a stand mixer fitted with a wire whisk attachment. Whisk in the soft butter in small increments at medium-low speed. Make sure each addition of butter is thoroughly incorporated before adding more butter. Scrape down the sides of the bowl with a spatula if necessary.

5. Once all of the butter is incorporated, adjust the mixer to medium-high speed. Continue to beat for a few more minutes until the white peach-chocolate cream is light and fluffy **(12)**.

Assembly and Decoration:

1. Fill a large piping bag (18 in/45.7 cm) fitted with a medium-sized plain tip (0.38 in/1 cm) with white peach-chocolate cream.

2. Place a bottom (larger) macaron disk on a clean surface with its smooth side down. Pipe dollops of cream along the outer edge of the macaron disk and in the center of the disk **(13–16)**.

3. Place fresh white peach pieces in the center **(17)**, followed by more cream **(18)**. Cover the filling with a top (smaller) macaron disk with its smooth side up **(19)**.

4. Pipe a dollop of cream on top of the pastry **(20)**; decorate the dessert with a chocolate curl and chocolate disk **(21–23)**.

PISTACHIO AND STRAWBERRY

Nothing says summer better than this classic pairing of pistachio and strawberry. This dessert takes on a whimsical ring shape with its filling exposed to showcase the vivid color contrast between fresh strawberries and the pistachio cream.

Fresh Strawberries

Mini Macaron Shells

Pistachios

Pistachio Mousseline Cream

Macaron Shell

Yield: 12 4-in/10.2-cm diameter ring-shaped individual desserts

INGREDIENTS

Macaron Shells:

1 recipe Macaron Shells (page 82); replace the blanched whole almonds with:

    2.65 oz/75 g raw shelled pistachios

+

    2.65 oz/75 g blanched whole almonds

Powdered sugar for dusting

Pistachio Mousseline Cream:

9.7 oz/275 g pastry cream (page 87)

3.53 oz/100 g pistachio paste

Macaron Shells:

1. Follow the directions on page 82 to make the batter for macaron shells. In step 3, replace the blanched whole almonds with a combination of raw shelled pistachios and blanched whole almonds **(1)**.

2. Dust the silicone baking mat with powdered sugar **(2)**; use a 2.75-in/7-cm round pastry cutter to make round impressions in the dusted sugar **(3)**.

3. Fill a large pastry bag (18 in/45.7 cm) fitted with a 0.38-in/1-cm plain tip with the macaron batter; pipe the batter along the circular outline in the dusted sugar to make a ring **(4)**. Pipe another ring of batter directly on top of the first ring to double the volume **(5)**. The batter will spread out to about 4 in/10.2 cm in diameter and 1.5 in/3.8 cm in width. Repeat to pipe more shells **(6)**.

1

2

Green gel food coloring (optional)

5.64 oz/160 g unsalted butter, at room temperature

Assembly and Decoration:

Fresh strawberries cut into wedges

Mini pistachio macaron shells

Toasted pistachios

4. Gently tap the baking pan against a hard surface to reduce air bubbles in the batter. Use a toothpick to pop any remaining air bubbles. Bake the macaron shells at 320°F/160°C for about 16 minutes.

5. Reserve some batter to pipe a half-sheet pan of mini macaron shells 1.25 in/3.2 cm in diameter (**7**). Bake the mini macaron shells at 325°F/163°C for about 11 minutes.

Pistachio Mousseline Cream:

1. Combine the pastry cream (page 87) with pistachio paste in a mixer bowl. Add a few drops of green food coloring if desired (**8**). Beat with a stand mixer fitted with a wire whisk attachment on medium-high speed until the mixture is smooth (**9**).

2. Reduce the mixer speed to medium-low, and whisk in the soft butter in small increments. Make sure each addition of butter is thoroughly incorporated before adding more butter. Scrape down the sides of the bowl with a spatula if necessary.

3. Once all of the butter is incorporated, adjust the mixer to medium-high speed. Continue to beat for a few more minutes until the cream is light and fluffy.

Assembly and Decoration:

1. Fill a large piping bag (18 in/45.7 cm) fitted with a medium-sized star tip (0.31 in/0.8 cm) with pistachio mousseline cream.

2. Place a macaron ring on a clean surface with its smooth side down. Pipe dollops of cream in two parallel rows on the macaron ring (**10, 11**).

3. Arrange fresh strawberry wedges and mini pistachio macaron shells on top of the cream (**12**). Sprinkle the dessert with toasted pistachios (**13**).

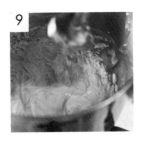

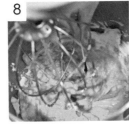

SUMMER SHOWPIECE

The macarons for this showpiece take on a different form than the familiar round shape. When arranged in a skewed pattern, these mini ladyfinger-shaped macarons resemble the woven pattern of a fruit basket. The showpiece is crowned with pulled sugar ribbon bows and decorated with sugar stems. It is the perfect centerpiece for any summer celebration.

INGREDIENTS

Macarons:

4 recipes Macaron Shells (page 82)

0.018 oz/0.5 g red + 0.0018 oz/0.05 g black powdered food coloring

0.007 oz/0.2 g red + 0.0007 oz/0.02 g blue powdered food coloring

0.018 oz/0.5 g green + 0.0018 oz/0.05 g yellow powdered food coloring

0.007 oz/0.2 g green + 0.0018 oz/0.05 g yellow powdered food coloring

Fillings for 4 recipes of macaron shells

Showpiece Structure:

1 12-in x 4-in/30.5-cm x 10.2-cm round Styrofoam disk (bottom tier)

1 8-in x 4-in/20.3-cm x 10.2-cm round Styrofoam disk (middle tier)

1 6-in x 4-in/15.2-cm x 10.2-cm round Styrofoam disk (top tier)

White drawing paper

Double-sided tape

Wooden toothpicks with two sharp ends

Macarons:

1. Follow the directions on page 82 to make four recipes of macaron batter. Use red, pink, green, and light green powdered food coloring mixtures in the batter to make four different colored macaron shells. Pipe the batter into 2-in/5.1-cm long strips (1–4). Bake the macaron shells at 320°F/160°C for about 13 minutes.

2. Fill the macaron shells with the fillings of your choice. The fillings should have a consistency that is neither too soft nor too hard. If the filling is too soft, the macarons will become soggy and fall off the showpiece structure; on the other hand, if the filling is too hard, it will be difficult to attach the macarons to the toothpicks.

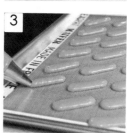

Showpiece Structure:

1. Cover the Styrofoam pieces with drawing paper using double-sided tape (5).

2. Insert toothpicks on one side of the middle tier Styrofoam disk (6). Apply a small amount of glue in the center of the bottom tier disk (7). Place the middle tier, with the toothpicks pointing downward, on top of the bottom tier and press down to stack the two layers. Repeat to stack the top tier (8).

3. For easy transport and enhanced stability, glue the supporting wooden board to the bottom of the lowest tier disk (9).

Nontoxic glue for arts and crafts

1 8-in x 0.5-in/20.3-cm x 1.3-cm round wooden board

Assembly and Decoration:

Sharp needle

Wooden toothpicks with two sharp ends

Pulled sugar decorations (page 95)

Assembly and Decoration:

1. Use a sharp needle to pierce a small hole in the bottom tier **(10)**. Insert a toothpick at the marked location at a 90° angle with respect to the surface of interest, leaving about 0.25-in/0.6-cm to 0.5-in/1.3-cm of the toothpick outside **(11)**. If the toothpick is too long, cut it in half and insert the cut side into the Styrofoam. Attach a macaron to the toothpick at a 45° angle **(12)**. **Note:** You may need two toothpicks to hold each macaron in place.

2. Repeat the process to attach more macarons to the supporting structure **(13)**. Each tier consists of two rows of macarons. If necessary, use a triangle ruler as a guide to align the macarons. Arrange the macarons in alternating colors **(14)**.

3. Attached pulled sugar decorations (page 95) to the showpiece with melted cooked sugar or isomalt sugar if desired.

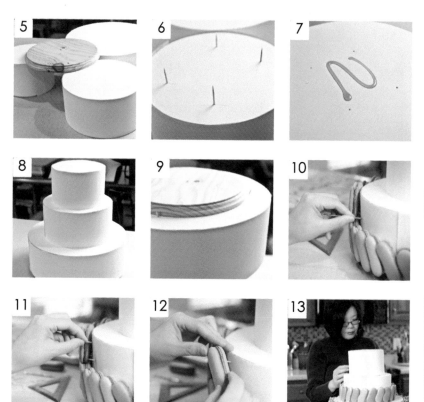

FALL

HAZELNUT, CRANBERRY, GINGER, AND RASPBERRY

This fun and festive dessert puts a smile on everyone's face. Bite into the rich and nutty hazelnut cream, and you will discover the sweet and tart cranberry cream with a surprising touch of fresh ginger. The raspberry garnishes remind you of the classic Linzer torte.

Mini Macaron Shells

Hazelnut Mousseline Cream

Fresh Raspberries

Cranberry & Ginger Cream

Macaron Shell

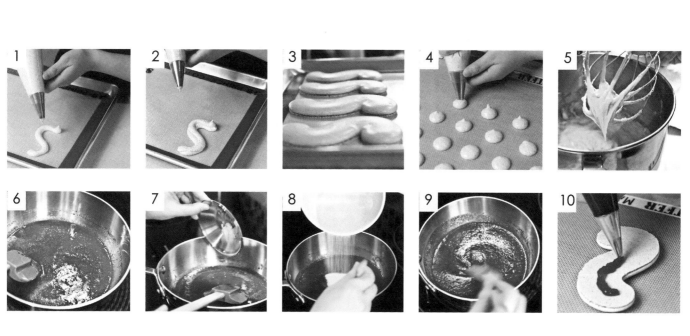

Yield: 16 4.5-in/11.4-cm S-shaped individual desserts

INGREDIENTS

Macaron Shells:

1 recipe Macaron Shells (page 82); replace the blanched whole almonds with:

5.29 oz/150 g whole natural hazelnuts

Hazelnut Mousseline Cream:

9.7 oz/275 g pastry cream (page 87)

3.53 oz/100 g hazelnut paste

5.64 oz/160 g unsalted butter, at room temperature

Cranberry and Ginger Cream:

3.53 oz/100 g granulated sugar

0.14 oz/4 g powdered pectin NH

7.05 oz/200 g cranberry puree

1.76 oz/50 g glucose syrup

0.11 oz/3 g grated fresh ginger

Assembly and Decoration:

Fresh raspberries

Powdered sugar

Mini hazelnut macaron shells

Macaron Shells:

1. Follow the directions on page 82 to make the batter for macaron shells. In step 3, replace the blanched whole almonds with whole natural hazelnuts.

2. Fill a large pastry bag (18 in/45.7 cm) fitted with a 0.38-in/1-cm plain tip with the macaron batter; pipe the batter into a 4-in/10.2-cm long S-shaped strip on the silicone baking mat (**1**); pipe another strip of batter directly on top of the first strip to double the volume (**2**). The batter will spread out to about 4.5 in/11.4 cm in length and 1.5 in/3.8 cm in width. Repeat to pipe more shells.

3. Gently tap the baking pan against a hard surface to reduce air bubbles in the batter. Use a toothpick to pop any remaining air bubbles. Bake the macaron shells at 320°F/160°C for about 15 minutes (**3**).

4. Reserve some batter to pipe a half-sheet pan of mini macaron shells 1.25 in/3.2 cm in diameter (**4**). Bake the mini macaron shells at 325°F/163°C for about 11 minutes.

Hazelnut Mousseline Cream:

1. Combine the pastry cream (page 87) with hazelnut paste in a mixer bowl. Beat with a stand mixer fitted with a wire whisk attachment on medium-high speed until the mixture is smooth.

2. Reduce the mixer speed to medium-low, and whisk in the soft butter in small increments. Make sure each addition of butter is thoroughly incorporated before adding more butter. Scrape down the sides of the bowl with a spatula if necessary.

3. Once all of the butter is incorporated, adjust the mixer to medium-high speed. Continue to beat for a few more minutes until the cream is light and fluffy (**5**).

Cranberry and Ginger Cream:

1. Combine the sugar and pectin in a mixing bowl. Mix thoroughly and reserve.

2. In a medium-sized stainless steel saucepan, combine cranberry puree, glucose syrup, and grated ginger (**6, 7**). Bring the mixture to a boil over medium-high heat. Stir in the sugar-pectin mixture (**8**). Bring the mixture back to a boil and reduce the heat to medium-low. Stir constantly and cook for another five minutes (**9**).

3. Let cool slightly. Cover the surface of the cranberry-ginger cream with plastic wrap. Allow the cream to cool completely before use.

Assembly and Decoration:

1. Fill a medium-sized piping bag (12 in/30.5 cm) fitted with a small plain tip (0.25 in/0.6 cm) with cranberry and ginger cream.

2. Place a macaron disk on a clean surface with its smooth side down. Pipe a row of cranberry and ginger cream along the center of the S-shaped macaron shell (**10**).

3. Fill a large piping bag (18 in/45.7 cm) fitted with a medium-sized plain tip (0.38-in/1-cm) with hazelnut mousseline cream. Pipe dollops of cream in two parallel rows above the cranberry and ginger cream (**11, 12**).

4. Place fresh raspberries on top of the cream and dust the raspberries with powdered sugar (**13, 14**). Arrange mini hazelnut macaron shells around the raspberries (**15**).

MEYER LEMON AND HAZELNUT

My parents have a few Meyer lemon trees in their home garden. Each fall, they send me boxes full of juicy, fragrant Meyer lemons. I use them in every application that I can think of, but my favorite dessert has to be the Meyer lemon macarons. The toasted hazelnuts add a crunchy element to the dessert, which results in a perfect balance with the sweet, citrusy Meyer lemon buttercream.

Chocolate Decoration

Macaron Shells

Meyer Lemon Buttercream

Hazelnut Halves

Chopped Hazelnuts

Yield: 6 to 8 4-in/10.2-cm diameter individual desserts

INGREDIENTS

Macaron Shells:

1 recipe Macaron Shells (page 82)

0.011 oz/0.3 g yellow + 0.0018 oz/0.05 g red powdered food coloring

Meyer Lemon Buttercream:

0.13 oz/3.8 g sheet gelatin (silver grade) or 0.11 oz/3.2 g powdered gelatin + 0.67 oz/19.2 g cold water

3.53 oz/100 g whole eggs

2.29 oz/65 g granulated sugar

2.82 oz/80 g Meyer lemon juice

0.25 oz/7 g fresh Meyer lemon zest from about 3 medium-sized Meyer lemons

1.41 oz/40 g unsalted butter, at room temperature

10.58 oz/300 g Swiss meringue buttercream (page 86)

Assembly and Decoration:

Toasted hazelnut halves and chopped hazelnut pieces

Chocolate decorations (page 90)

Macaron Shells:

1. Follow the directions on page 82 to make the batter for macaron shells. Add powdered food coloring if desired.

2. To make the large macaron shell disks, fill a large pastry bag (18 in/45.7 cm) fitted with a 0.38-in/1-cm plain tip with the macaron batter, and pipe a 3.5-in/8.9-cm disk by making a spiral coil on the silicone baking mat (1). The batter will spread out to about 4 in/10.2 cm in diameter. Repeat to pipe more shells.

3. Gently tap the baking pan against a hard surface to reduce air bubbles in the batter. Use a toothpick to pop any remaining air bubbles (2). Bake the macaron shells at 320°F/160°C for about 16 to 18 minutes (3, 4).

Meyer Lemon Buttercream:

1. In a medium-sized bowl, bloom the sheet gelatin in plenty of cold water. If powdered gelatin is used, sprinkle the powder over 0.66 oz/19.2 g cold water in the bowl. Let the gelatin bloom for at least 10 minutes before use.

2. Combine eggs and granulated sugar in a stainless steel mixing bowl. Mix well with a balloon whisk. Set aside.

3. Heat the Meyer lemon juice and lemon zest in a medium-sized stainless steel saucepan over medium-high heat (5). Remove from heat when the mixture comes to a boil. Pour about half of the mixture into the reserved egg mixture while whisking vigorously (6). Pour the entire mixture back into the pan. Cook the mixture over medium-low heat while whisking constantly for about one to two minutes until the mixture thickens (7).

4. Press the mixture through a mesh strainer into a mixing bowl to remove the lemon zest (8, 9). Stir in the butter and mix well (10).

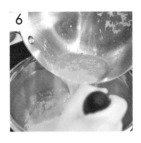

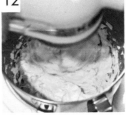

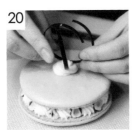

5. Meanwhile, squeeze excess water out of the bloomed sheet gelatin and add the gelatin to the Meyer lemon mixture (11). If powdered gelatin is used, add the entire content to the Meyer lemon mixture. Stir to combine. Cover the surface of the mixture with plastic wrap.

6. When the mixture has cooled completely, combine it with Swiss meringue buttercream (page 86) in a mixer bowl. Beat with a stand mixer fitted with a wire whisk attachment on high speed until the Meyer lemon buttercream is light, fluffy, and well combined (12).

Assembly and Decoration:

1. Fill a large piping bag (18 in/45.7 cm) fitted with a large star tip (0.56 in/1.4 cm) with Meyer lemon buttercream.

2. Place a macaron disk on a clean surface with its smooth side down. Pipe dollops of buttercream along the outer edge of the macaron disk and in the center of the disk (13–15).

3. Place toasted hazelnut halves between dollops of cream along the edge (16); sprinkle chopped hazelnut pieces in the center (17). Cover the filling with another macaron disk with its smooth side up (18).

4. Pipe a dollop of cream on top of the pastry (19). Finish decorating the dessert with a chocolate disk and curls (20, 21).

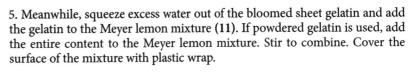

APPLE, CARAMEL, AND CINNAMON CRUMBLE

The classic flavors of autumn are transformed into this marvelous macaron dessert. Sweet and velvety caramel cream, crispy and juicy apples, crunchy and buttery cinnamon crumble, all packed in between two elegant macaron shells. I can't think of another autumn dessert that is so familiar and comforting, yet so stylish.

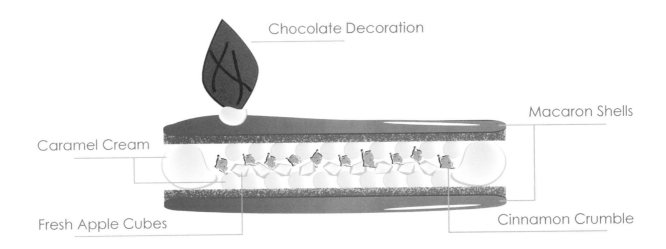

Chocolate Decoration

Macaron Shells

Caramel Cream

Fresh Apple Cubes

Cinnamon Crumble

 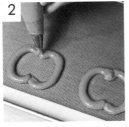 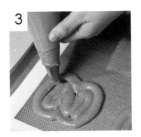  

Yield: 6 to 8 4.5-in/11.4-cm diameter apple-shaped individual desserts

INGREDIENTS

Macaron Shells:

1 recipe Macaron Shells (page 82)

0.021 oz/0.6 g red + 0.0018 oz/0.05 g yellow powdered food coloring

Caramel Cream:

0.088 oz/2.5 g sheet gelatin (silver grade) or 0.074 oz/2.1 g powdered gelatin + 0.44 oz/12.6 g cold water

1.76 oz/50 g granulated sugar (A)

2.82 oz/80 g heavy whipping cream

Pinch of salt

1.41 oz/40 g egg yolks

0.88 oz/25 g granulated sugar (B)

0.63 oz/18 g cornstarch

7.05 oz/200 g whole milk

0.88 oz/25 g granulated sugar (C)

4.94 oz/140 g unsalted butter, at room temperature

Cinnamon Crumble:

1.76 oz/50 g all-purpose flour

1.76 oz/50 g almond flour

1.06 oz/30 g granulated sugar

0.71 oz/20 g Turbinado sugar

0.018 oz/0.5 g cinnamon powder

Pinch of salt

Macaron Shells:

1. Follow the directions on page 82 to make the batter for macaron shells. Add powdered food coloring if desired.

2. To make the large macaron shell shaped like an apple, fill a large pastry bag (18 in/45.7 cm) fitted with a 0.38-in/1-cm plain tip with the macaron batter, and pipe the outline of an apple approximately 4.5 in x 4 in/11.4 cm x 10.2 cm on the silicone baking mat (**1, 2**). Pipe more batter inside the frame to fill the apple shape (**3**). Repeat to pipe more shells.

3. Gently tap the baking pan against a hard surface to reduce air bubbles in the batter. Use a toothpick to pop any remaining air bubbles. Bake the macaron shells at 320°F/160°C for about 16 to 18 minutes (**4**).

Caramel Cream:

1. In a medium-sized bowl, bloom the sheet gelatin in plenty of cold water. If powdered gelatin is used, sprinkle the powder over 0.44 oz/12.6 g cold water in the bowl. Let the gelatin bloom for at least 10 minutes before use.

2. To make the caramel sauce, place the sugar (A) in a medium-sized stainless steel saucepan and dry melt the sugar over medium heat (**5**). Stir occasionally until a medium-dark amber color is achieved (at about 356°F/180°C) (**6**). Carefully monitor the cooking process to avoid burning the caramel.

3. Meanwhile, heat the heavy whipping cream in a small saucepan on the stovetop or in a microwave oven.

4. When the caramel has reached the desired consistency, add warm cream to the caramel (**7**). Stir vigorously and continue to cook the caramel sauce for one to two minutes until the caramel sauce reaches 226°F/108°C (**8, 9**). Smooth out any lumps, add salt, and stir again to combine (**10**). Reserve the caramel sauce.

1.76 oz/50 g unsalted butter cubes, chilled

Assembly and Decoration:

Fresh apple pieces, cut into 0.25-in/0.6-cm cubes

Chocolate decorations (page 90)

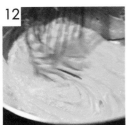

5. To make the custard, first combine egg yolks, sugar (B), and cornstarch in a stainless steel mixing bowl. Mix well with a balloon whisk. Set aside.

6. Heat the milk and sugar (C) in a medium-sized stainless steel saucepan over medium-high heat. Remove from heat when the milk comes to a boil. Pour about half of the hot liquid into the reserved egg yolk mixture while whisking vigorously (**11**). Pour the entire mixture back into the pan. Cook the custard mixture over medium-low heat while whisking constantly for about one to two minutes until the custard thickens (**12**).

7. Meanwhile, squeeze excess water out of the bloomed sheet gelatin and add the gelatin to the custard (**13**). If powdered gelatin is used, add the entire content to the custard. Stir to combine. Add the reserved caramel sauce and mix well (**14, 15**). Press the mixture through a mesh strainer to eliminate any lumps (**16**). Cover the surface of the caramel-custard mixture with plastic wrap.

8. Place the caramel-custard mixture in a mixer bowl when it has cooled completely. Attach the bowl to a stand mixer fitted with a wire whisk attachment. Whisk in the soft butter in small increments at medium-low speed. Make sure each addition of butter is thoroughly incorporated before adding more butter. Scrape down the sides of the bowl with a spatula if necessary.

9. Once all of the butter is incorporated, adjust the mixer to medium-high speed. Continue to beat for a few more minutes until the caramel cream is light and fluffy (**17**).

Cinnamon Crumble:

1. Combine flour, almond flour, granulated sugar, Turbinado sugar, cinnamon powder, and salt in a food processor bowl. Pulse the machine a few times to evenly distribute the ingredients (**18**). Add the chilled butter cubes (**19**). Pulse the machine a few more times until small pea-sized dough pieces are formed (**20, 21**). Do not over-mix.

2. Line a baking sheet with parchment paper, spread the dough pieces on top of the parchment paper (22). Place the baking sheet in the freezer for about five minutes or in the refrigerator for about 30 minutes to chill the dough pieces.

3. Meanwhile, preheat the oven to 350°F/177°C. Remove the baking sheet from the freezer. Bake the cinnamon crumble for about 10 to 15 minutes until golden brown (23). Let cool completely and reserve.

Assembly and Decoration:

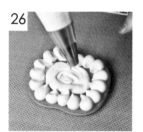

1. Fill a large piping bag (18 in/45.7 cm) fitted with a medium-sized plain tip (0.38-in/1-cm) with caramel cream.

2. Place a macaron disk on a clean surface with its smooth side down. Pipe dollops of cream along the outer edge of the macaron disk and in the center of the disk (24–26).

3. Place fresh apple cubes in the center, and follow with apple crumble (27, 28). Pipe some cream on the dull and flat side of another macaron disk (29). Place it on top of the filling (30).

4. Pipe a dollop of cream on top of the pastry (31). Decorate with a chocolate leaf (32).

FALL SHOWPIECE

When I was about ten years old, I saw a photograph of Frank Lloyd Wright's Fallingwater with the most splendid autumn foliage as its backdrop. The image stuck in my mind as the most picture perfect autumn scene. In this showpiece, I attempted to capture the mood of that photo using a foliage-inspired color palette and macarons as my media. I think my interpretation of the Fallingwater is pleasing to both the eye and the palate.

INGREDIENTS

Macarons:

3 recipes Macaron Shells (page 82)

0.021 oz/0.6 g yellow + 0.0018 oz/0.05 g red powdered food coloring

0.028 oz/0.8 g red + 0.0035 oz/0.1 g yellow + 0.0018 oz/0.05 g black powdered food coloring

0.011 oz/0.3 g black + 0.011 oz/0.3 g red + 0.0035 oz/0.1 g yellow powdered food coloring

Fillings for 3 recipes of macaron shells

Showpiece Structure:

2 14-in x 8-in x 3-in/35.6-cm x 20.3-cm x 7.6-cm rectangular Styrofoam blocks

2 15-in x 7.5-in x 3-in/38.1-cm x 19.1-cm x 7.6-cm rectangular Styrofoam blocks

White and/or beige drawing paper

Double-sided tape

Wooden toothpicks with two sharp ends

Nontoxic glue for arts and crafts

Macarons:

1. Follow the directions on page 82 to make three recipes of 1.5-in/3.8-cm macaron shells. Use yellow, red, and brown powdered food coloring mixtures in the batter to make three different colored macaron shells (1–3).

2. Fill the macaron shells with the fillings of your choice (4). The fillings should have a consistency that is neither too soft nor too hard. If the filling is too soft, the macarons will become soggy and fall off the showpiece structure; on the other hand, if the filling is too hard, it will be difficult to attach the macarons to the toothpicks.

Showpiece Structure:

1. Cover the Styrofoam pieces with drawing paper using double-sided tape (5).

2. Insert toothpicks on one side of one Styrofoam block (6). Apply a small amount of glue in the center of another block (7). Place the first block, with the toothpicks pointing downward, on top of the second block and press down to stack the two layers. If desired, stack the tiers on a slight offset. Repeat to stack the top two tiers (8).

3. For easy transport and enhanced stability, glue the supporting wooden boards to the bottom of the lowest tier (9).

3 4-in x 4-in x 0.5-in/10.2-cm x 10.2-cm x 1.3-cm square wooden boards

Assembly and Decoration:

Sharp needle

Wooden toothpicks with two sharp ends

Chocolate decorations (page 90)

Tempered dark chocolate (page 90)

Parchment paper cornet

Cooling spray for sugar and chocolate

Assembly and Decoration:

1. Use a sharp needle to pierce a small hole in the bottom tier (**10**). Insert a toothpick at the marked location at an 80° to 90° angle with respect to the surface of interest, leaving about 0.25-in/0.6-cm to 0.5-in/1.3-cm of the toothpick outside (**11**). If the toothpick is too long, cut it in half and insert the cut side into the Styrofoam. Attach a macaron to the toothpick (**12**).

2. Repeat the process to attach more macarons to the supporting structure (**13**). Each tier consists of two rows of macarons. If necessary, use a ruler as a guide to align the macarons. Arrange the macarons in alternating colors (**14**).

3. To decorate the showpiece with chocolate leaves (page 90), put tempered chocolate into a parchment paper cornet, apply a small amount of chocolate on the back of a leaf (**15**), and attach it to the showpiece. If desired, spray the attaching joint with cooling liquid to solidify the chocolate instantly (**16**). Repeat to add more chocolate leaves. Place three chocolate flowers (made from chocolate leaves) on top of the showpiece.

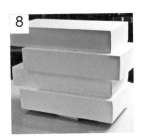

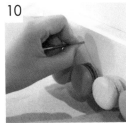

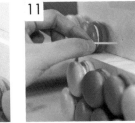

WINTER

WINTER

PEANUT

The ordinary peanut is transformed into a sophisticated and whimsical macaron dessert. Instead of the typical round shape, I created these peanut macaron shells to resemble the shape of a peanut shell. I think after just one taste, you will be delighted and amused by this charming macaron creation.

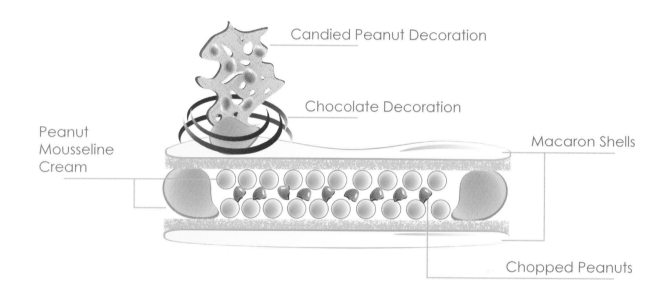

Candied Peanut Decoration

Chocolate Decoration

Peanut Mousseline Cream

Macaron Shells

Chopped Peanuts

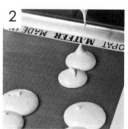

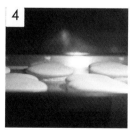

Yield: 10 5.5-in/14-cm long individual desserts

INGREDIENTS

Macaron Shells:

1 recipe Macaron Shells (page 82); replace the blanched whole almonds with:

   5.29 oz/150 g raw blanched peanuts

Peanut Mousseline Cream:

9.7 oz/275 g pastry cream (page 87)

4.23 oz/120 g peanut butter

5.64 oz/160 g unsalted butter, at room temperature

Assembly and Decoration:

Roasted peanuts, coarsely chopped

Whole roasted peanuts

7.05 oz/200 g isomalt sugar granules

0.71 oz/20 g distilled water

Chocolate decorations (page 90)

Macaron Shells:

1. Follow the directions on page 82 to make the batter for macaron shells. In step 3, replace the blanched whole almonds with raw blanched peanuts.

2. Fill a large pastry bag (18 in/45.7 cm) fitted with a 0.69-in/1.7-cm plain tip with the macaron batter. Pipe the batter into a 2.25-in/5.7-cm mound on the silicone baking mat (1); pipe another mound with a bigger diameter (3 in/7.6 cm) about 1.5 in/3.8 cm below the first mound (2). The batter will spread out and two circular mounds will overlap to resemble the peanut shape. Repeat to pipe more shells (3).

3. Gently tap the baking pan against a hard surface to reduce air bubbles in the batter. Use a toothpick to pop any remaining air bubbles. Bake the macaron shells at 320°F/160°C for about 16 minutes (4, 5).

Peanut Mousseline Cream:

1. Combine the pastry cream (page 87) with peanut butter in a mixer bowl. Beat with a stand mixer fitted with a wire whisk attachment on medium-high speed until the mixture is smooth.

2. Reduce the mixer speed to medium-low, and whisk in the soft butter in small increments. Make sure each addition of butter is thoroughly incorporated before adding more butter. Scrape down the sides of the bowl with a spatula if necessary.

3. Once all of the butter is incorporated, adjust the mixer to medium-high speed. Continue to beat for a few more minutes until the cream is light and fluffy (6).

Assembly and Decoration:

1. Fill a large piping bag (18 in/45.7 cm) fitted with a medium-sized plain tip (0.38-in/1-cm) with peanut mousseline cream.

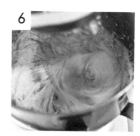

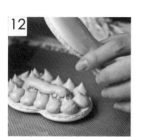

2. Place a macaron disk on a clean surface with its smooth side down. Pipe dollops of cream along the outer edge of the macaron disk and in the center of the disk (7–9).

3. Sprinkle chopped peanuts in the center and then pipe more cream on top of the peanuts (10, 11). Cover the filling with another macaron disk with its smooth side up (12, 13).

4. To make the peanut-bubble sugar decoration, spread out whole roasted peanuts on a piece of parchment paper on a heat-proof flat surface. In a medium-sized saucepan, cook the isomalt sugar granules and water over medium-high heat until the liquid reaches 356°F/180°C. Immediately pour the hot isomalt liquid on top of the peanuts. Hold the edges of the parchment paper and shake the paper gently to allow the isomalt liquid to flow over the peanuts and create the bubbling effect. Let cool completely. Break the candy into small pieces.

5. Pipe a dollop of cream on top of the pastry (14). Decorate the dessert with chocolate curls and peanut-bubble sugar (15, 16).

CHOCOLATE AND SPICE

This is a chocolate and macaron lover's dream dessert. Dark chocolate cream that is full of intense cocoa flavor, and packed with the essence of ginger, cardamom, cinnamon, and vanilla. It's also the perfect cure for those winter blues.

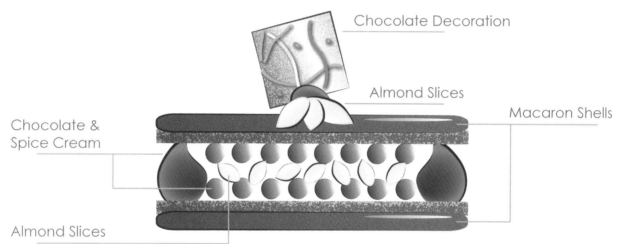

Chocolate Decoration

Almond Slices

Macaron Shells

Chocolate & Spice Cream

Almond Slices

Yield: 10 to 12 3.25-in/8.3-cm square individual desserts

INGREDIENTS

Macaron Shells:

1 recipe Macaron Shells (page 82)

0.018 oz/0.5 g black + 0.007 oz/0.2 g yellow + 0.007 oz/0.2 g red powdered food coloring

Unsweetened cocoa powder for dusting

Chocolate and Spice Cream:

7.05 oz/200 g whole milk

0.35 oz/10 g sliced fresh ginger

3 whole cardamom pods, cut into halves

1 cinnamon stick

1 vanilla bean

1.41 oz/40 g egg yolks

1.76 oz/50 g granulated sugar

0.63 oz/18 g cornstarch

4.23 oz/120 g bittersweet dark chocolate couverture, finely chopped

0.71 oz/20 g unsalted butter, at room temperature (A)

4.23 oz/120 g unsalted butter, at room temperature (B)

Assembly and Decoration:

Toasted almond slices

Chocolate decorations (page 90)

Macaron Shells:

1. Follow the directions on page 82 to make the batter for macaron shells (**1**). Add powdered food coloring if desired.

2. Dust the silicone baking mat with unsweetened cocoa powder (**2**); use a 2.5-in/6.4-cm square pastry cutter to make square impressions in the dusted sugar (**3, 4**).

3. Fill a large pastry bag (18 in/45.7 cm) fitted with a 0.38-in/1-cm plain tip with the macaron batter; pipe the batter inside the square frame in a zig-zag pattern (**5, 6**). The batter will spread out to a 3.25-in/8.3-cm square (approximately). Repeat to pipe more shells (**7**).

4. Gently tap the baking pan against a hard surface to reduce air bubbles in the batter. Use a toothpick to pop any remaining air bubbles. Lightly dust each macaron shell with more cocoa powder on top if desired (**8, 9**). Bake the macaron shells at 320°F/160°C for about 16 minutes.

Chocolate and Spice Cream:

1. Combine milk, ginger slices, cardamom pods, and cinnamon stick in a medium-sized stainless steel saucepan. Use a paring knife to split the vanilla bean lengthwise. Scrape off the vanilla seeds using the back of the knife. Add the vanilla bean halves and seeds to the saucepan (**10**). Bring the mixture to a boil. Remove from heat. Cover the pan and allow the mixture to infuse for about 20 minutes.

2. Meanwhile, combine egg yolks, sugar, and cornstarch in a stainless steel mixing bowl. Mix well with a balloon whisk. Set aside.

3. To make the chocolate-spice pastry cream, bring the milk and spice infusion back to a boil. Remove from heat and strain the mixture using a mesh strainer to remove the aromatics (**11**). Pour the infused milk over the reserved egg yolk mixture

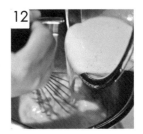

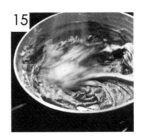

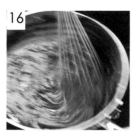

while whisking vigorously **(12)**. Pour the entire mixture back into the pan. Cook the mixture over medium-low heat while whisking constantly for about one to two minutes until the mixture thickens **(13)**. Remove from heat.

4. Stir in the dark chocolate pieces and mix well **(14, 15)**. Stir in the soft butter (A) and mix vigorously until the mixture is smooth and homogenous **(16)**. Cover the surface of the chocolate-spice pastry cream with plastic wrap.

5. Place the chocolate-spice pastry cream in a mixer bowl when it has cooled completely. Attach the bowl to a stand mixer fitted with a wire whisk attachment. Whisk in the soft butter (B) in small increments at medium-low speed. Make sure each addition of butter is thoroughly incorporated before adding more butter. Scrape down the sides of the bowl with a spatula if necessary.

6. Once all of the butter is incorporated, adjust the mixer to medium-high speed. Continue to beat for a few more minutes until the chocolate and spice cream is light and fluffy **(17)**.

Assembly and Decoration:

1. Fill a large piping bag (18 in/45.7 cm) fitted with a medium-sized plain tip (0.38-in/1-cm) with chocolate and spice cream.

2. Place a macaron disk on a clean surface with its smooth side down. Pipe dollops of cream along the outer edge of the macaron disk and in the center of the disk **(18–21)**.

3. Sprinkle almond slices in the center, and then pipe more cream on top of the almonds **(22, 23)**. Cover the filling with another macaron disk with its smooth side up **(24)**.

4. Pipe a dollop of cream on top of the pastry **(25)**. Decorate the dessert with a chocolate square and more almond slices **(26)**.

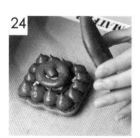

WALNUT, FIG, AND CHOCOLATE

When I was a little girl, I used to help my grandmother in the kitchen. She loved to play baroque music in the background while we were at work. One time she asked me to crack some walnuts when Vivaldi's *Four Seasons* concertos were playing. I remember that I would "attack" the walnuts feverishly with a small hammer during the fast-tempo first movement of the winter concerto, and then I would take a break during the slower *Largo* movement. To this day, I think of walnuts whenever I hear Vivaldi's winter concerto. This dessert is nothing short of a "macaron masterpiece" composed of the perfect ensemble of walnut, fig, and chocolate cream.

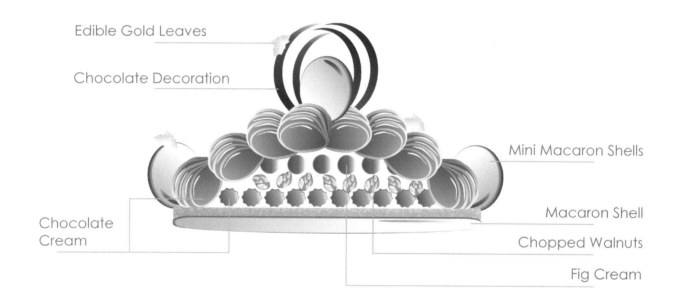

Edible Gold Leaves

Chocolate Decoration

Mini Macaron Shells

Chocolate Cream

Macaron Shell

Chopped Walnuts

Fig Cream

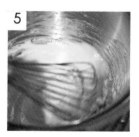

Yield: 6 to 8 5-in/12.7-cm diameter individual desserts

Macaron Shells:

1 recipe Macaron Shells (page 82); replace the blanched whole almonds with:

    2.12 oz/60 g walnut pieces

    +

    3.17 oz/90 g blanched whole almonds

Chocolate Cream:

1.41 oz/40 g egg yolks

0.88 oz/25 g granulated sugar (A)

0.63 oz/18 g cornstarch

7.05 oz/200 g whole milk

0.88 oz/25 g granulated sugar (B)

1.41 oz/40 g bittersweet chocolate couverture, finely chopped

2.82 oz/80 g milk chocolate couverture, finely chopped

0.71 oz/20 g unsalted butter, at room temperature (A)

5.64 oz/160 g unsalted butter, at room temperature (B)

Fig Cream:

0.13 oz/3.8 g sheet gelatin (silver grade) or 0.11 oz/3.2 g powdered gelatin + 0.67 oz/19.2 g cold water

9.52 oz/270 g fig puree

1.06 oz/30 g granulated sugar

0.49 oz/14 g cornstarch

Macaron Shells:

1. Follow the directions on page 82 to make the batter for macaron shells. In step 3, replace the blanched whole almonds with a combination of walnut pieces and blanched whole almonds.

2. To make the large macaron shell disks, fill a large pastry bag (18 in/45.7 cm) fitted with a 0.38-in/1-cm plain tip with the macaron batter, and pipe a 4.25-in/10.8-cm disk by making a spiral coil on the silicone baking mat (**1**). The batter will spread out to about 5 in/12.7 cm in diameter. Repeat to pipe more shells (**2**).

3. Gently tap the baking pan against a hard surface to reduce air bubbles in the batter. Use a toothpick to pop any remaining air bubbles. Bake the macaron shells at 320°F/160°C for about 16 to 18 minutes.

4. Reserve some batter to pipe a half-sheet pan of mini macaron shells 1.25 in/3.2 cm in diameter (**3**). Bake the mini macaron shells at 325°F/163°C for about 11 minutes (**4**).

Chocolate Cream:

1. Combine egg yolks, sugar (A), and cornstarch in a stainless steel mixing bowl. Mix well with a balloon whisk (**5**). Set aside.

2. To make the chocolate pastry cream, place the milk and sugar (B) in a medium-sized stainless steel saucepan. Heat the milk mixture over medium-high heat. Remove from heat when it comes to a boil. Pour about half of the hot liquid into the reserved egg yolk mixture while whisking vigorously (**6**). Pour the entire mixture back into the pan (**7**). Cook the mixture over medium-low heat while whisking constantly for about one to two minutes until the mixture thickens (**8**). Remove from heat.

3. Stir in the dark and milk chocolate pieces and mix well (**9, 10**). Stir in the soft butter (A) and mix vigorously until the mixture is smooth and homog-

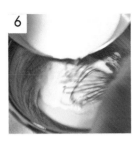

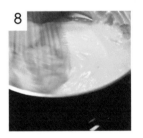

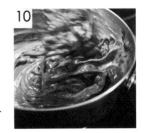

Assembly and Decoration:

Toasted walnut pieces

Chocolate decorations (page 90)

Mini walnut macaron shells

Edible gold leaves

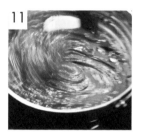

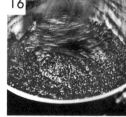

enous **(11, 12)**. Cover the surface of the chocolate pastry cream with plastic wrap.

4. Place the chocolate pastry cream in a mixer bowl when it has cooled completely. Attach the bowl to a stand mixer fitted with a wire whisk attachment. Whisk in the soft butter (B) in small increments at medium-low speed. Make sure each addition of butter is thoroughly incorporated before adding more butter. Scrape down the sides of the bowl with a spatula if necessary.

5. Once all of the butter is incorporated, adjust the mixer to medium-high speed. Continue to beat for a few more minutes until the chocolate cream is light and fluffy **(13)**.

Fig Cream:

1. In a medium-sized bowl, bloom the sheet gelatin in plenty of cold water. If powdered gelatin is used, sprinkle the powder over 0.67 oz/19.2 g cold water in the bowl. Let the gelatin bloom for at least 10 minutes before use.

2. Combine the fig puree, sugar, and cornstarch in a medium-sized stainless steel saucepan. Mix well with a balloon whisk. Bring the mixture to a boil over medium-high heat while whisking constantly **(14)**. Remove from heat when the mixture thickens. Let cool slightly.

3. Meanwhile, squeeze excess water out of the bloomed sheet gelatin and add the gelatin to the fig mixture **(15)**. If powdered gelatin is used, add the entire content to the fig mixture. Stir to combine **(16)**. Let cool slightly. Cover the surface of the fig cream with plastic wrap. Let cool completely.

Assembly and Decoration:

1. Fill a large piping bag (18 in/45.7 cm) fitted with a medium-sized star tip (0.31 in/0.8 cm) with chocolate cream.

2. Place a macaron disk on a clean surface with its smooth side down. Pipe dollops of chocolate

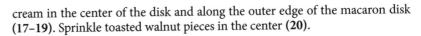

cream in the center of the disk and along the outer edge of the macaron disk (**17–19**). Sprinkle toasted walnut pieces in the center (**20**).

3. Fill a medium-sized piping bag (12 in/30.5 cm) fitted with a small plain tip (0.25 in/0.6 cm) with fig cream; pipe some cream in the center (**21**).

4. Switch back to the large pastry bag filled with chocolate cream and pipe two more layers of chocolate cream in the center (**22, 23**).

5. Place chocolate curls on top of the dessert (**24**). Arrange mini walnut macaron shells along the outer edge of the dessert and place one mini macaron shell inside the chocolate curls (**25–27**). Finish decorating the dessert with a few pieces of edible gold leaves on top if desired (**28, 29**).

WINTER SHOWPIECE

This showpiece captured the mood of a wintry landscape in which clear blue skies, snow-blanketed fields, and sparkling icicles are recreated using macarons and sugar. This dazzling showpiece will make you wish that winter would come earlier.

Ingredients

Macarons:

3 recipes Macaron Shells (page 82)

0.0071 oz/0.2 g white powdered food coloring

0.011 oz/0.3 g blue powdered food coloring

0.028 oz/0.8 g blue powdered food coloring

Fillings for 3 recipes of macaron shells

Showpiece Structure:

1 14-in x 14-in x 3-in/35.6-cm x 35.6-cm x 7.6-cm square Styrofoam block (bottom tier)

1 12-in x 10-in x 3-in/30.5-cm x 25.4-cm x 7.6-cm rectangular Styrofoam block (middle tier)

1 8-in x 8-in x 4-in/20.3-cm x 20.3-cm x 10.2-cm square Styrofoam block (top tier)

White drawing paper

Double-sided tape

Wooden toothpicks with two sharp ends

Nontoxic glue for arts and crafts

1 12-in x 9-in x 0.5-in/30.5-cm x 22.9-cm x 1.3-cm rectangular wooden board

Assembly and Decoration:

Sharp needle

Macarons:

1. Follow the directions on page 82 to make three recipes of 1.5-in/3.8-cm macaron shells. Use white, light blue and blue powdered food coloring in the batter to make three different colored macaron shells (1–3).

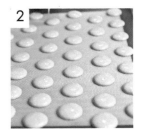

2. Fill the macaron shells with the fillings of your choice (4). The fillings should have a consistency that is neither too soft nor too hard. If the filling is too soft, the macarons will become soggy and fall off the showpiece structure; on the other hand, if the filling is too hard, it will be difficult to attach the macarons to the toothpicks.

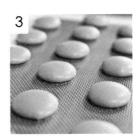

Showpiece Structure:

1. Cover the Styrofoam pieces with drawing paper using double-sided tape (5).

2. Insert toothpicks on one side of the middle tier Styrofoam block (6). Apply a small amount of glue in the center of the bottom tier (7). Place the middle tier, with the toothpicks pointing downward, on top of the bottom tier and press down to stack the two layers. Repeat to stack the top tier (8).

3. For easy transport and enhanced stability, glue the supporting wooden board to the bottom of the lowest tier (9).

Assembly and Decoration:

1. Use a sharp needle to pierce a small hole in the bottom tier (10). Insert a toothpick at the marked

Wooden toothpicks with two sharp ends

Pulled sugar decorations (page 95)

location at an 80° to 90° angle with respect to the surface of interest, leaving about 0.25-in/0.6-cm to 0.5-in/1.3-cm of the toothpick outside **(11)**. If the toothpick is too long, cut it in half and insert the cut side into the Styrofoam. Attach a macaron to the toothpick **(12)**.

2. Repeat the process to attach more macarons to the supporting structure **(13)**. Each of the bottom two tiers contains two rows of macarons and the top tier contains three rows of macarons **(14)**. If necessary, use a ruler as a guide to align the macarons.

3. Attached pulled sugar decorations (page 95) to the showpiece with melted cooked sugar or isomalt sugar if desired.

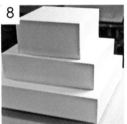

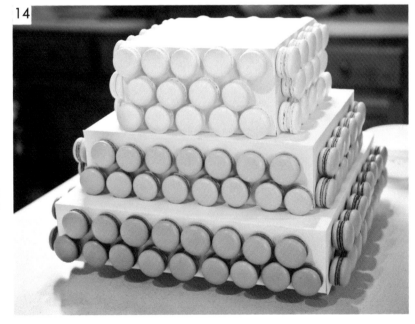

BASIC RECIPES

BASIC RECIPES

MACARON SHELLS

This recipe provides basic instructions on how to make macaron shells. Although several variations have been mentioned throughout the book, the underlying technique can be applied in all cases. The three key factors that determine the success of the final product are temperature, moisture, and viscosity. We explore methods for precisely controlling these factors and how to use them to our advantage.

Yield: Shells for about 45 1.5-in/3.8-cm filled macarons, 6 to 8 4-in/10.2-cm diameter individual desserts, or 65 1.25-in/3.2-cm filled mini macarons

INGREDIENTS

2 oz/57 g aged egg whites (about 2 egg whites), at room temperature

5.29 oz/150 g blanched whole almonds or blanched almond flour

5.29 oz/150 g granulated sugar

Powdered food coloring, water soluble (optional)

7.41 oz/210 g Italian meringue (page 85)

Macaron Shells (1.5-in/3.8-cm):

1. On the day before baking, separate the eggs and place the egg whites in a mixing bowl. Loosely cover the bowl with plastic wrap and refrigerate overnight. Reserve the yolks for another use.

2. One hour before baking, take the aged egg whites out of the refrigerator and allow them to return to room temperature.

3. Meanwhile, combine blanched whole almonds and sugar (**1**). Process the almond-sugar mixture in a food processor for about 15 seconds or until the mixture becomes a fine powder (**2, 3**). If almond flour is used, combine the almond flour and sugar. Process the mixture in a food processor for a few seconds to pulverize the sugar and eliminate the lumps in the almond flour. Do not over-mix. Pour the mixture into a medium-sized mixing bowl and reserve.

4. Mix the powdered food coloring (if used) with the aged egg whites (**4**). Add the colored egg whites to the reserved almond-sugar mixture (**5**). Mix all ingredients well with a spatula or bowl scraper until a thick, sticky paste has formed (**6**). Set aside.

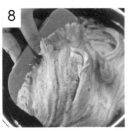

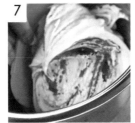

5. Follow the instructions on page 85 to make the Italian meringue. Mix the Italian meringue with the almond-sugar paste using a spatula or bowl scraper; mix until a soft, glossy batter forms. When lifted up with the spatula, the batter should flow back into the bowl in ribbons, and the ribbons should disappear in about 10 to 18 seconds (7–10).

6. Preheat a conventional oven to 325°F/163°C (reduce the temperature to 300°F/149°C if a convection oven is used). Line a 13-in x 18-in/33-cm x 45.7-cm half-sheet pan with a half-sheet-sized silicone baking mat.

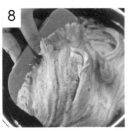

7. Fill a large pastry bag (18 in/45.7 cm) fitted with a 0.38-in/1-cm plain tip with the macaron batter (11, 12). Pipe the mixture into 1-in/2.5-cm mounds, with 1-in/2.5-cm spacing, on the silicone baking mat (13). The mixture will spread out to about 1.5-in/3.8-cm in diameter.

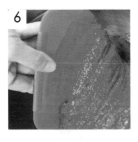

8. Gently tap the baking pan against a hard surface to reduce air bubbles in the batter. Use a toothpick to pop any remaining air bubbles (14). Bake the macaron shells for about 12 minutes on the upper rack in the oven (15). Remove the baking pan from the oven and place it on a cooling rack (16).

9. Let the macaron shells cool completely before removing them from the silicone mat. Place them on a large clean surface with the smooth side up. Flip over half of the shells and pipe the filling onto the shells using a medium-sized (12-in/30.5-cm) pastry bag (17, 18). Cover the piped filling with the remaining shells to make sandwiches (19, 20).

10. Refrigerate the macarons overnight before serving. The macarons will stay fresh for about 3 to 4 days in the refrigerator or about 3 to 4 weeks stored in the freezer. Serve at room temperature.

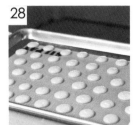

Large Macaron Shells (4-in/10.2-cm):

1. Follow the instructions for making macaron shells from steps 1 through 4.

2. Follow the instructions on page 85 to make the Italian meringue. Mix the Italian meringue with the almond-sugar paste using a spatula or bowl scraper; mix until a soft, glossy batter forms. The batter for large macaron shells requires less mixing. When lifted up with the spatula, the batter should flow back into the bowl in ribbons, and the ribbons should disappear in about 20 seconds to 1 minute.

3. To make the large macaron shell disks, fill a large pastry bag (18 in/45.7 cm) fitted with a 0.38-in/1-cm plain tip with the macaron batter, and pipe a 3.5-in/8.9-cm disk by making a spiral coil on the silicone baking mat **(21)**. The batter will spread out to about 4 in/10.2 cm in diameter. Repeat to pipe more shells **(22)**.

4. Gently tap the baking pan against a hard surface to reduce air bubbles in the batter. Use a toothpick to pop any remaining air bubbles **(23)**. Bake the macaron shells at 320°F/160°C for about 16 to 18 minutes **(24, 25)**.

5. Let the macaron shells cool completely before removing them from the silicone mat. Follow the specific instructions for each recipe to complete the process of making each individual dessert.

Mini Macaron Shells (1.25-in/3.2-cm):

Follow the instructions for making macaron shells except in step 7, pipe the mixture into 0.75-in/1.9-cm mounds on the silicone baking mat **(26, 27)**. The mixture will spread out to about 1.25-in/3.2-cm in diameter **(28)**. In step 8, bake the mini macaron shells at 325°F/163°C for about 11 minutes **(29, 30)**.

ITALIAN MERINGUE

Italian meringue is one of the key components in macaron shells. The success of the macaron shells depends on the consistency of the Italian meringue. When executed correctly, Italian meringue will give the macaron shells that slight chewiness and much needed substance to support the filling on top. This recipe makes enough Italian meringue for two recipes of macaron shells. This is particularly convenient if you are making two types of macaron shells, in which case you can divide the meringue into two equal portions. If you are making one recipe of macaron shells, you can reserve half of the Italian meringue for other uses, for instance, in an Italian meringue buttercream or to lighten a mousse.

Yield: About 14.81 oz/420 g Italian meringue

INGREDIENTS

4 oz/113 g fresh egg whites (about 4 egg whites), at room temperature

0.035 oz/1 g dried egg white powder

10.58 oz/300 g granulated sugar

2.65 oz/75 g distilled water

1. For the Italian meringue, place the fresh egg whites in a 5-qt/4.7-L mixer bowl. Add the dried egg white powder and stir the egg white mixture slightly. Attach the mixer bowl to the mixer fitted with the wire whisk attachment (1, 2).

2. Cook the sugar and water in a saucepan over medium-high heat. Stir constantly until the sugar has dissolved. When the mixture comes to a boil, insert a candy thermometer and stop stirring (3). When the sugar syrup reaches 230°F/110°C, turn on the mixer and start to beat the egg whites at high speed.

3. When the sugar syrup reaches 244°F/118°C, remove the saucepan from the heat. By now, the egg whites should have formed foamy, soft peaks and tripled in volume (4). Slowly pour the syrup in a steady stream along the sides of the mixer bowl while the mixer is whisking (5). Continue to beat until stiff, glossy peaks form and the meringue has cooled to about 95°F/35°C (6, 7). Depending on the ambient temperature, it will take about 10 to 15 minutes' whisking on high speed for the meringue to cool down and achieve the desired consistency.

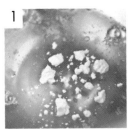

SWISS MERINGUE BUTTERCREAM

Swiss meringue buttercream is light, creamy, and delicious. In this book, we use Swiss meringue buttercream as the base for several fillings. This recipe makes enough buttercream for about two types of macaron desserts.

Yield: About 21.16 oz/600 g buttercream

INGREDIENTS

4 oz/113 g fresh egg whites (about 4 egg whites), at room temperature

7.05 oz/200 g granulated sugar

12 oz/340 g unsalted butter, at room temperature

1. Combine egg whites and sugar in a 5-qt/4.7-L mixer bowl (**1**). Place the bowl over a saucepan filled with simmering water over medium-low heat.

2. Beat the egg whites and sugar with a balloon whisk constantly until the mixture reaches 160°F/71°C (**2, 3**).

3. Remove the mixer bowl from the water bath, and attach the bowl to the mixer fitted with the wire whisk attachment. Beat the mixture on high speed until stiff, glossy peaks form and the meringue has cooled to room temperature (**4, 5**).

4. Reduce the mixer speed to medium-low, and whisk in the soft butter in small increments (**6**). Make sure each addition of butter is completely incorporated into the meringue before adding more butter. Scrape down the sides of the bowl with a spatula if necessary.

5. Once all of the butter is incorporated, adjust the mixer to medium-high speed. Continue to beat for a few more minutes until the buttercream is light and fluffy (**7, 8**).

6. Place the buttercream in a container. Cover the surface of the buttercream directly with plastic wrap. Store in the refrigerator if not used immediately. Use the buttercream at room temperature.

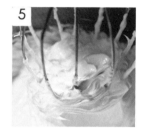

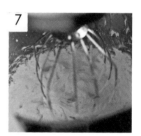

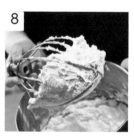

PASTRY CREAM

The simple technique and versatile applications make pastry cream one of the essential components in a pastry kitchen. In this book, we use pastry cream as the base for several filling recipes. This recipe makes enough pastry cream for two types of macaron desserts.

Yield: About 20.46 oz/580 g pastry cream

INGREDIENTS

2.82 oz/80 g egg yolks

1.76 oz/50 g granulated sugar (A)

1.06 oz/30 g cornstarch

14.11 oz/400 g whole milk

1.76 oz/50 g granulated sugar (B)

1 vanilla bean

1.06 oz/30 g unsalted butter, at room temperature

1. Combine egg yolks, sugar (A), and cornstarch in a stainless steel mixing bowl **(1)**. Mix well with a balloon whisk **(2)**. Set aside.

2. Place the milk and sugar (B) in a medium-sized stainless steel saucepan. Use a paring knife to split the vanilla bean lengthwise. Scrape off the vanilla seeds using the back of the knife. Add the vanilla bean halves and seeds into the saucepan.

3. Heat the milk mixture over medium-high heat **(3)**. Remove from heat when it comes to a boil. Remove the vanilla bean halves. Pour about ⅓ of the hot liquid into the reserved egg yolk mixture while whisking vigorously **(4, 5)**. Pour the entire mixture back into the pan **(6)**. Cook the mixture over medium-low heat while whisking constantly for about one to two minutes until the mixture thickens **(7, 8)**. Let cool slightly. Stir in the soft butter and mix well.

4. Cover the surface of the pastry cream with plastic wrap. Store in the refrigerator if not used immediately. Use at room temperature.

  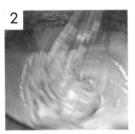  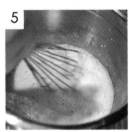
  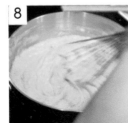

DECORATING TECHNIQUES

DECORATING TECHNIQUES

CHOCOLATE DECORATIONS

Chocolate and sugar decorations symbolize the highest degree of pastry-making skill. Mastering the artistry to create these stunning works of edible art takes years of training and practice. Chocolate work requires patience, clean organization, careful planning, meticulous execution, and most of all a thorough understanding of the material's properties. To achieve the desired glossy appearance and firm texture in chocolate decorations, it is absolutely essential to work with properly tempered or crystallized chocolate. The best method for small batch tempering is called "seeding," in which small amounts of solid chocolate pieces are introduced to melted chocolate to help reconstruct the proper crystallized formation. The use of colored cocoa butter creates an entirely new means of artistic expression in chocolate decoration. In this book, we employ two types of cocoa butter application techniques. In the first method, the colored cocoa butter is sprayed or painted over an acetate sheet or polycarbonate mold, followed by a thin layer of tempered chocolate. This method creates a pointillist effect on a shiny, glossy surface. In the second method, the colored cocoa butter is sprayed over solid dark chocolate squares to create a velvety appearance.

INGREDIENTS

Colored cocoa butter for pastry work

17.64 oz/500 g or desired amount of bittersweet dark chocolate couverture, finely chopped

Special Equipment and Tools:

Acetate sheets for pastry work

Spray gun (preferably gravity-feed) equipped with a compressor

Chocolate warmer/melter (optional)

Large offset spatula

Plastic or cardboard tubes for shaping the chocolate decorations

Pastry cutters for forming uniformly shaped chocolate decorations

Colored Cocoa Butter Application:

1. Cut the acetate sheets into half-sheet-size (about 13 in x 18 in/33 cm x 45.7 cm) rectangular pieces.

2. Heat the colored cocoa butter in a microwave oven for about 20 seconds. Stir with a spoon and heat another 20 seconds. Repeat the process until the cocoa butter is completely melted and the temperature is between 95°F/35°C and 100°F/38°C.

3. Let the cocoa butter cool slightly; when its temperature drops to 87°F/31°C, pour the cocoa butter into the spray gun, and lightly spray the acetate sheets (1, 2). Spray the acetate sheets with a second layer of cocoa butter of a different color if desired. Do not over-spray and cover the acetate sheets completely with the cocoa butter paints.

4. Let the cocoa butter solidify slightly. If desired, use the corner of a plastic dough scraper to make random lines on the cocoa butter (3–5).

5. Let the cocoa butter solidify completely before continuing to the next step.

Note: You can paint the colored cocoa butter on the acetate sheets with a clean

Polycarbonate half-sphere chocolate mold for making chocolate spheres

Parchment paper cornet

Cooling spray for sugar and chocolate

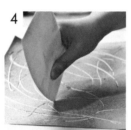

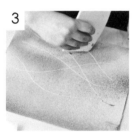

paint brush instead of a spray gun. Although you will not be able to see the pointillist effect if a brush is used, the appearance of the final result will still be impressive.

Chocolate Tempering or Crystallization:

To temper or crystallize the chocolate using a double boiler:

1. Add water to a small saucepan until about ⅓ full, and let simmer over low heat. Place a mixing bowl on top of the saucepan. Choose a mixing bowl that fits snugly on top of the saucepan; the bottom of the bowl must not touch the water. Place about 75% of the chocolate pieces into this water bath and reserve the rest of the chocolate pieces for seeding **(6)**.

2. Stir the chocolate with a spatula and monitor the temperature carefully **(7, 8)**. When the temperature reaches 120°F/49°C, take the mixing bowl off the saucepan. Do not heat the chocolate above 130°F/54°C and do not let any water drop into the chocolate.

3. Allow the melted chocolate to cool to 115°F/46°C. Add the remaining seeding chocolate pieces gradually and stir occasionally with a spatula **(9)**. When the temperature drops to 90°F/32°C, the chocolate is ready for use **(10)**.

To temper or crystallize the chocolate using a chocolate melter:

1. Place about 75% of the chocolate pieces into the melter and reserve the rest of the chocolate pieces for seeding. Set the machine at around 130°F/54°C.

2. When the chocolate pieces are completely melted and the temperature reaches around 120°F/49°C, reduce the melter's temperature setting to 90°F/32°C.

3. Allow the melted chocolate to cool to 115°F/46°C. Add the remaining seeding chocolate pieces grad-

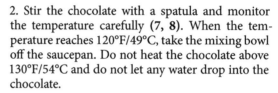

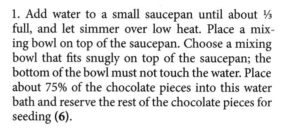

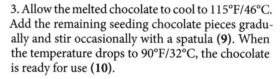

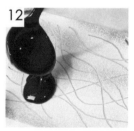

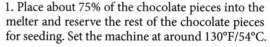

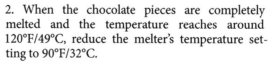

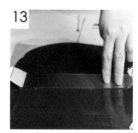

ually and stir occasionally with a spatula. When the temperature drops to 90°F/32°C, the chocolate is ready for use (**11**).

Note: If all of the chocolate pieces are melted before the temperature drops below 95°F/35°C, add a small amount of solid chocolate pieces and stir. On the other hand, if any solid chocolate pieces remain after the temperature drops to 90°F/32°C, remove with a spoon.

Chocolate Leaf Decorations:

1. Place a sprayed acetate sheet on a clean, flat work surface with the cocoa butter painted side facing up.

2. Pour a small amount of tempered chocolate on the acetate sheet (**12**); immediately spread out the chocolate with an offset spatula into an even, thin layer (**13, 14**).

3. Let the chocolate solidify slightly. If the chocolate was properly crystallized, it should start to set in a few minutes.

4. As soon as the chocolate turns from glossy to matte, make a test cut on the corner. If the cut comes out clean, continue to cut out the desired design shapes, such as leaves, using a paring knife (**15–17**). Work quickly before the chocolate becomes too firm to make clean cuts. In addition to freehand designs, you can use a pastry cutter to cut out uniform shapes.

5. Let the chocolate leaves solidify completely before removing them from the acetate sheets (**18, 19**). Store the chocolate decorations in an airtight container in a cold, dark, and dry place until ready to use.

Variations:

Curved Leaves: After the chocolate leaves are cut, place a piece of parchment paper on top. Immediately roll the entire acetate sheet, with the chocolate leaves and parchment paper on top, around a plastic or cardboard tube. Secure and hold the acetate sheet in place with tape. Let the chocolate leaves solidify completely before removing from the acetate sheet. The leaves will take on the curved shape of the tube (**20**).

Round Disks: Follow the directions for making the chocolate leaves; in step 4, use a round pastry cutter to cut out circular disks instead of freehand designs (**21–23**).

Squares: For chocolate squares with a velvety appearance and embossed designs, the process follows a reversed order. First, spread the tempered dark chocolate on a clean piece of acetate sheet. Cut out squares using a paring

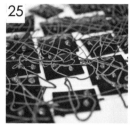

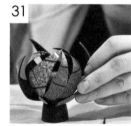

knife and ruler. After the chocolate squares are solidified, fill a parchment paper cornet with tempered milk chocolate, pipe some random lines and dots on the glossy side of the chocolate squares (and bring out your inner Jackson Pollock). When the designs are solidified, spray the squares with white cocoa butter (**24–26**).

Spheres: Spray a half-sphere polycarbonate chocolate mold with colored cocoa butter (**27, 28**). Let the cocoa butter set completely. Pour tempered dark chocolate into the mold. Gently tap the mold against a hard surface to remove trapped air bubbles. Wait for 10 seconds and pour out the excess chocolate from the mold. Scrape the surface of the mold with a scraper to clean it. When the chocolate half-spheres are solidified, remove from the mold (**29**). Slightly melt the open-end of a half sphere, and attach it to another half sphere to form a complete sphere.

Flowers: To make a flower from the curved leaves, put tempered chocolate into a parchment paper cornet, apply a small amount of chocolate on the back of a leaf, and attach it to a round chocolate base. If desired, spray the attaching joint with cooling liquid to solidify the chocolate instantly (**30**). Repeat to add more chocolate leaves until a flower is formed (**31, 32**).

PULLED SUGAR DECORATIONS

Just like chocolate decoration, sugar work requires clean organization, careful execution, an intimate knowledge of the material, and an understanding of its various workable states. Because of its unique characteristics, sugar work also requires a certain degree of artistic spontaneity, creative intuition, and dexterity. Manipulating hot sugar is difficult. The sugar is always either too hot or too cold to work with, and when you finally have the perfect texture, the sugar just will not cooperate. When I first started to make sugar decorations, I noticed the similarities between sugar work and glass blowing. I found a documentary film on the glass artistry of Dale Chihuly, which features his collaborative projects with the Venetian masters Lino Tagliapietra and Pino Signoretto. I watched the film dozens of times to study the working process of glass blowing and sculpting, and then I realized that the "secret" to glass blowing and sugar work is *gravity*! Yes, gravity. The physical law that makes Newton's apple fall causes Earth to orbit around the Sun and governs the entire universe. When you let gravity do its work, the sugar will bend and fall naturally, and you can "catch" it at the right moment to curl, stretch, and twist the sugar in the most natural fashion.

A word of caution on working with sugar: Because the optimal working temperature of sugar can cause serious burns, be sure to wear protective gloves at all times. If there are any blisters on your hands after working with sugar, keep them clean and cover with a bandage to prevent infection.

INGREDIENTS

35.27 oz/1000 g granulated sugar

14.11 oz/400 g distilled water

2.82 oz/80 g glucose syrup

Candy thermometer

0.026 oz/0.75 g tartaric acid solution (equal portions of tartaric acid granules and water by weight)

Gel paste food coloring or powdered food coloring dissolved in a small amount of water

Special Equipment and Tools:

Sugar Cooking Process:

1. Combine the sugar and water in a 1.9-qt/1.8-L copper or stainless steel saucepan. Heat the mixture over medium heat. Stir with a spatula constantly until the sugar is dissolved; skim off any impurities or foam that flow to the top (**1**).

2. When the sugar syrup comes to a boil, stir in the glucose syrup (**2**). Bring the mixture back to a boil.

3. Insert the candy thermometer and stop stirring. Increase the heat to medium-high. Continue to cook the sugar; brush down the sides of the pan with a pastry brush dipped in cold water to prevent sugar crystals from forming (**3**).

Silicone baking mats

Sugar gloves or latex gloves (powder-free)

Heating lamps for sugar work

Propane torch

Glass alcohol lamp

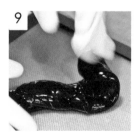

4. Cook the sugar until it reaches 333°F/167°C, about 20 minutes' cooking time (**4**). Remove from heat, add the tartaric acid solution, and stir to combine (**5**). Return the pan to the heat and continue to cook until the sugar reaches 342°F/172°C (**6**). Remove from the heat.

5. Add the desired food coloring and mix to combine (**7**).

Note: You can make several colors from the same batch of cooked sugar. If the colors have similar hues but with different intensities (e.g., yellow, light yellow green, dark yellow green), you can add the lightest color to the sugar first. Mix well and pour out the desired amount. Then add the second lightest color, mix well, and pour out the desired amount of the second color. Repeat to finish the third color. If the colors are from the opposite sides of the spectrum, you will need to separate the sugar into different pans first and mix in the colors separately.

6. Immediately pour the cooked sugar onto silicone baking mats on a heat-proof surface (**8**).

Preparing the Sugar:

1. Let the sugar cool for a few minutes, and start to fold the outer edges of the sugar into itself to allow even cooling.

Note: Cooked sugar at high temperatures can cause serious burns. Wear protective gloves at all times when working with cooked sugar.

2. Continue to fold the sugar into itself until it is cold enough to be stretched. Shape the sugar into a rope and hold it up with both of your hands. Start to pull and fold to incorporate air; the sugar will turn opaque and shiny (**9–11**). When it has an elastic resistant feel and a satin-like appearance, it is ready to be used. Keep the sugar pieces warm and pliable under heating lamps.

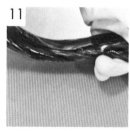

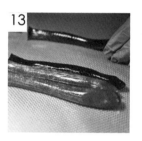

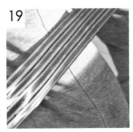

Pulled Sugar Ribbons:

1. Cut off a piece of sugar and roll it into a rope with the palms of your hands. Repeat the process for other colors of sugar pieces.

2. Arrange the sugar ropes of different colors next to each other in a desired color pattern to make a wide piece of ribbon (12, 13). Press the ends of the ribbon to make sure the ropes are sticking together.

3. Pick up the ribbon and evenly stretch it until it is about two to three times its original length (14). Fold the ribbon in half and stick the two ends side-by-side so that the ribbon is doubled in width and the original color pattern is duplicated (15). Slightly stretch and flatten the folding point.

4. Repeat the stretching and folding process one or two more times (16–18). After the final fold, stretch the ribbon into the final desired length (19).

5. Place the ribbon on a flat surface. Heat a knife or stainless steel scraper with a propane torch. Cut the ribbon into segments using the hot scraper (20, 21).

6. To form a bow, hold a piece of ribbon under the heating lamp for a few seconds until the ribbon bends slightly (22, 23). Pinch both ends of the ribbon and bend it into a bow (24–26). Set aside to let it cool. Repeat to make more bows (27).

7. To assemble the bows into a single piece, first make a round disk out of cooked sugar; heat the end of a sugar bow using a glass alcohol lamp (28, 29), stick the bow onto the round disk, and hold the bow in place until the melted sugar hardens. Repeat to attach more bows to the disk to finish a complete ribbon-bow sugar piece (30).

8. Let it cool completely. Store the sugar decoration in an airtight container in a cold, dark, and dry place until ready to use. If desired, place some silica gel or limestone desiccant next to the sugar pieces in the container to reduce humidity.

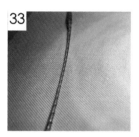

Variations:

Pulled Sugar Stems: Combine thin ropes of sugar pieces of different colors into one rope, and start to twist and stretch it with the palms of your hands on a flat surface (**31, 32**). Continue to twist and stretch until the desired thickness is obtained (**33**). Cut the long stem into stem segments, warm the segments under a heating lamp, and bend them into the desired shape (**34, 35**). Heat the end of a sugar stem using a glass alcohol lamp and attach the stem to the sugar decoration (**36**),

Pulled Sugar Flower: Hold the edge of a large piece of sugar and pull out a flower petal; cut off the petal with a pair of scissors. Curl the tip-end of the petal when it is still pliable and pinch the root-end of the petal slightly. Repeat to make more petals. To assemble the flower, first make a round disk out of cooked sugar; heat the root-end of a petal using a glass alcohol lamp, stick the petal onto the round disk, and hold the petal in place until the melted sugar hardens. Repeat to attach more petals to the disk to finish a complete pulled sugar flower.

LIST OF RESOURCES

I think the best method for locating hard-to-find ingredients and baking tools is to conduct an internet search. For your reference, I have included a list of the stores where I shopped for the ingredients and tools used in this book.

For Pastry Equipment and Tools:

Amazon.com (www.amazon.com)
Chef Rubber (www.chefrubber.com)
JB Prince (www.jbprince.com)
Kerekes (www.bakedeco.com)
King Arthur Flour (www.kingarthurflour.com)
Pastry Chef Central (www.pastrychef.com)
Sur la Table (www.surlatable.com)
Williams-Sonoma (www.williams-sonoma.com)

For Pastry Ingredients:

Adagio Teas (www.adagio.com): loose tea leaves
Amazon.com (www.amazon.com): general pastry ingredients
American Almond Products Company (www.americanalmond.com): wholes nuts and nut flours
Arizona Vanilla Company (www.arizonavanilla.com): vanilla beans
Chef Rubber (www.chefrubber.com): general pastry ingredients, powdered food coloring
The Chefs' Warehouse (www.chefswarehouse.com): general pastry ingredients
Hamlovers (www.hamlovers.com): jamón ibérico de bellota
Honeyville Food Products (www.honeyvillegrain.com): almond flours, dried egg whites
King Arthur Flour (www.kingarthurflour.com): general pastry ingredients
L'Epicerie (www.lepicerie.com): fruit purees
La Tienda (www.tienda.com): Spanish saffron, jamón ibérico de bellota
Marky's (www.markys.com): fruit purees
Pastry Chef Central (www.pastrychef.com): general pastry ingredients
Sambazon (www.sambazon.com): açaí puree
Teavana (www.teavana.com): loose tea leaves
World Wide Chocolate (www.worldwidechocolate.com): chocolates

MACARON MAGIC

Jialin Tian, Ph.D.

Photographs & Design by Jialin Tian
Step-by-Step Photographs by Yabin Yu

MACARON MAGIC (BOOK 1)

YABIN

READY FOR MACARONS!

CPSIA information can be obtained
at www.ICGtesting.com
Printed in the USA
LVIW02n0833260713
344530LV00002BA